ECDL

EUROPEAN COMPUTER DRIVING LICENCE

ECDL

EUROPEAN COMPUTER DRIVING LICENCE

Moira Stephen

TEACH YOURSELF BOOKS

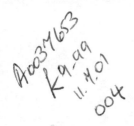

Aoo3\7653
K9-99
K 11.4.01
004

For UK orders: please contact Bookpoint Ltd, 78 Milton Park, Abingdon, Oxon OX14 4TD. Telephone: (44) 01235 400414, Fax: (44) 01235 400454. Lines are open 9.00 – 6.00, Monday to Saturday, with a 24-hour message answering service. E-mail address: orders@bookpoint.co.uk

For USA and Canada orders: please contact NTC/Contemporary Publishing, 4255 West Touhy Avenue, Lincolnwood, Illinois 60646-1975, USA. Telephone: (847) 679 5500, Fax: (847) 679 2494.

Long renowned as the authoritative source for self-guided learning – with more than 40 million copies sold worldwide – the *Teach Yourself* series includes over 200 titles in the fields of languages, crafts, hobbies, business and education.

British Library Cataloguing in Publication Data
A catalogue record for this title is available from the British Library.

Library of Congress Catalog Card Number: On file.

First published in UK 2001 by Hodder Headline Plc, 338 Euston Road, London, NW1 3BH.

First published in US by NTC/Contemporary Publishing, 4255 West Touhy Avenue, Lincolnwood (Chicago), Illinois 60646-1975 USA.

The 'Teach Yourself' name and logo are registered trade marks of Hodder & Stoughton Ltd. Computer hardware and software brand names mentioned in this book are protected by their respective trademarks and are acknowledged.

Copyright © 2001 Moira Stephen

Typeset by MacDesign, Southampton
Printed in Great Britain for Hodder & Stoughton Educational, a division of Hodder Headline Plc, 338 Euston Road, London NW1 3BH by Cox & Wyman, Reading, Berkshire.

Impression number	10 9 8 7 6 5 4 3 2 1
Year	2006 2005 2004 2003 2002 2001

CONTENTS

PREFACE

In the preface we will:

- introduce the ECDL and explain the structure of the award
- suggest a route to the award
- discuss the Logbook
- help you find your local test centre
- summarize the tests
- give an overview of this book
- suggest useful Web addresses.

What is ECDL?

ECDL stands for European Computer Driving Licence. The ECDL is an internationally accepted qualification. The objective of the ECDL programme is to promote and encourage computer literacy for all by:

- raising the level of knowledge about Information Technology (IT)
- encouraging a higher level of basic personal computer (PC) competence and improved standards in the use of common computer applications
- increasing awareness of 'best practices' and the advantages of PCs
- providing a basic qualification that will allow people to demonstrate that they are part of the 'Information Society'.

The ECDL is deployed and monitored by the European Computer Driving Licence Foundation (ECDL-F). The role of the Foundation is to promote and co-ordinate the development of the ECDL concept. Its role has now developed to cover the International Computer Driving Licence (ICDL) – the name given to the qualification outside Europe.

The Council of European Professional Informatics Societies (CEPIS) supports and approves the qualification in Europe. The British Computer

Society (BCS) is the body that has implemented and now administers ECDL in the UK.

The key to ECDL is that it provides a standardized proof of competence – across Europe and now internationally through the ICDL.

How does it work?

The qualification consists of seven modules, one theory (Module 1, *Basic Concepts of Information Technology*) and six practical (Modules 2–7). Each module has a test that you must sit and pass if you want the full licence. All the tests should normally be completed within three years of registration for the programme. It doesn't matter what order you take the tests in, nor does it matter where you take them. You can sit the tests in any approved centre in the UK, Europe or internationally. You don't need to take all your tests in the same centre.

The modules are:

1. Basic Concepts of Information Technology (IT)
2. Using the Computer and Managing Files
3. Word Processing
4. Spreadsheets
5. Database
6. Presentation
7. Information and Communication

Where do I start?

This book is as good a place as any! It covers everything you need for each module and gives mock tests so that you can check your level of competence.

You can do the modules in ANY order - it really is up to you. If you're not sure which order you should do the modules in I suggest you:

♦ Read Chapter 1, *Basic Concepts of Information Technology*. This chapter discusses the theory that will be tested in Module 1 and introduces some of the jargon you will meet in the other modules. Either do the Module 1 test after reading Chapter 1, or leave it until you've used a computer for a while (you may find discussing applications, e-mail and the Internet easier once you've used them).

- Do Module 2, *Using the Computer and Managing Files* (Chapter 2). It provides information on skills that will be useful no matter what application, e.g. word processing, database, spreadsheet, etc. that you go on to use.

- Work on the other practical modules in whatever order you wish. You could start with an application that you already use. Or, you could choose one that you feel will be most useful in the early stages of using your computer, e.g. *Word Processing* or *Information and Communications*.

- Go back to Module 1, *Basic Concepts of Information Technology* (if you haven't already done it). If you've left this one till the end, you'll find that the practical experience you've gained working on the other modules is useful. Read through Chapter 1 again and try the mock tests before you do the Module 1 ECDL test.

European Computer Logbook

When you register for ECDL either with your local test centre (you'll find information on test centres at hyperlink **http://www.bcs.org.uk**) or directly with the BCS, you will be issued with a European Computer Logbook. You need your Logbook each time you do a test. The document is used to officially record details of the tests that you sit and pass. When you have completed all seven tests, you (or your test centre) should send your Logbook to the BCS where it will be exchanged for your ECDL.

The tests

You must sit your tests at an approved test centre.

When you feel ready to sit a test, contact your local test centre to arrange your assessment. You should take proof of identity with you, e.g. driving licence or passport, when you go for your test.

You must have a European Computer Logbook before taking a test (if you don't have one the test centre will be able to issue one). If you successfully pass the test, the Test Centre will sign your Logbook and record that you have passed.

Tests will be taken under exam conditions. All test materials will be issued to you at the beginning of the test and you must hand everything back at the end of it. You are allowed to use on-line help, but you are not allowed to use books or notes during the test. Each test lasts 45 minutes.

Module 1 (Basic Concepts of Information Technology (IT)) – the test consists of eight open-ended questions. The first six questions are worth four marks each, the last two are worth three marks each. If a question is worth four marks, you should make four different points in your answer, three marks needs three different points mentioned. You must score a minimum of 18/30 (60%) to pass the test.

Module 2 (Using the Computer and Managing Files) – the test consists of 15 tasks. Two marks are allocated for each task in the test. You must score a minimum of 24/30 (80%) to pass the test.

Module 3 (Word Processing) – the test consists of 30 tasks, each worth one mark. You must score a minimum of 24/30 (80%) to pass the test.

Module 4 (Spreadsheets) – the test consists of 30 tasks. The task to set up a spreadsheet is worth four marks, and all others are worth one mark each. You must score a minimum of 24/30 (80%) to pass the test.

Module 5 (Database) – the test is in two parts. Setting up a database – you will be asked to set up a database with five fields, and to enter three records. One mark is given for each field set up correctly and one mark is given for each record entered correctly. All other tasks are each worth one mark. Querying an existing database – there will be 15 tasks, each worth one mark. You must score a minimum of 24/30 (80%) to pass the test.

Module 6 (Presentation) – the test is in two parts. Part one tests your ability to create a presentation file, part two tests your ability to modify an existing presentation file. Each part is worth 15 marks. You must score a minimum of 24/30 (80%) to pass the test.

Module 7 (Information and Communication) – the test is in two parts. Part one tests your ability to use the Internet, part two tests your ability to use an e-mail package. Each part is worth 15 marks. You must score a minimum of 24/30 (80%) to pass the test.

Candidate Disk

When you sit your test, a Candidate Disk will be provided for the tests in Modules 2–7. Support files and folders, work files or an answer file will be on this disk (as appropriate to the test). You must hand this disk back to the tester at the end of your test.

Answer file

If you are asked to describe an operation or procedure or to give factual information you must type your response into an answer file that will be provided in the Answer folder on your Candidate Disk.

Using this book

This book consists of eight chapters:

1. Basic concepts of Information Technology (IT)
2. Using the computer and managing files
3. Word processing
4. Spreadsheets
5. Databases
6. Presentations
7. Information and communication
8. Common skills

You can use the book on its own to find out about IT and learn how to use the applications required in the ECDL programme or you may use it as a text book to support a course you are following at school, college or work.

Although you can do ECDL tests on any computer with suitable software, this book is based on the use of a PC with Windows 95 or Windows 98, Microsoft Office, Internet Explorer and Outlook Express.

There is a mock test at the end of each of chapters 1–7.

Chapter 1, *Basic Concepts of Information Technology*, discusses the theory required for the Module 1 test.

Chapter 2, *Using the Computer and Managing Files*, covers those basic computer skills required for the Module 2 test. You will find that the knowledge gained in this chapter is useful in all the other ECDL modules, so I suggest you do this one before Modules 3–7.

Chapter 3 covers the material for the *Word Processing* test, Module 3.

Chapter 4 covers the material for the *Spreadsheet* test, Module 4.

Chapter 5 covers the material for the *Database* test, Module 5.

Chapter 6 covers the material for the *Presentations* test, Module 6.

Chapter 7 covers the material for the *Information and Communication* test, Module 7.

Chapter 8, *Common Skills*, discusses those routines that are similar in all applications, e.g. save, print, format, spell check, etc. You will probably find (at least initially) that you use this chapter *plus* the chapter for the particular application you are studying.

Mock tests

The mock tests at the end of chapters 1–7 are similar to what you might expect in the ECDL test. I suggest you attempt them before going for your real test. Remember to time yourself (45 minutes maximum), and don't use any notes or books to help.

Useful web sites

For more information on ECDL visit:

www.bcs.org.uk – go to ECDL from the home page. You'll find information about test centres and also sample test questions at this site.

www.ecdl.com

I hope you find this book useful when preparing for your ECDL tests and wish you every success.

Moira Stephen

2001

1 | BASIC CONCEPTS OF INFORMATION TECHNOLOGY

AIMS OF THIS CHAPTER

In this chapter we will discuss the basic physical make-up of a personal computer and some of the basic concepts of Information Technology (IT). Topics include hardware, different types of computer, the different parts of a computer, software – operating system and applications, and system development. We also discuss information networks and IT in society. Health and safety issues, system security and legal issues associated with computers will also be covered.

1.1 Getting started

Hardware, Software and Information Technology

Hardware refers to any *physical* parts of a computer. The visual display unit (VDU) or monitor, printer, keyboard, mouse, trackball, storage devices (hard drive, diskette), speakers, central processing unit, electronic components, boards, memory chips, etc. are all items of hardware.

Software refers to the *programs* that make your computer work. Software includes the operating system (essential to get your computer up and running) and the application software, e.g. software that lets you carry out specific tasks (word processing, spreadsheets, e-mail, database, etc.).

Information Technology (IT) refers to any means of storing, processing and transmitting information using modern technology (computers). The term *Information and Communication Technology* (ICT) has also emerged. ICT encompasses facsimile, telephone, multimedia presentations, etc. as well as computers.

Types of computer

Personal Computer (PC)

The type of computer that you are most likely to use is the PC. Originally the PC was developed and marketed by a company called IBM. Launched in 1981 it became a great success, so much so that other companies copied it and marketed their own PC 'clones' as IBM-compatible PCs.

The PC consists of a monitor, keyboard, mouse and a box containing the electronics, hard drive, memory, etc. The box may be under the monitor (in a desktop model), or it may be standing beside it or on the floor under it (if the box is a tower model).

Laptop

As people began to rely more on their PC for business and personal use, the demand for a portable PC grew. This led to the development of laptops – smaller PCs powered by batteries that could be carried about in a briefcase. The batteries would only work for a few hours before they had to be recharged – which meant you might need to take the charger with you (and perhaps a spare battery). Portable printers were designed so that you could print out your work while you were out and about, and, if you wanted to send/receive data and faxes, a cellular phone (connected to your laptop using an interface card and cable) could be used. A large (pretty large) briefcase would be needed to carry all this hardware – useful, but perhaps a less 'portable' solution than it first appeared.

Palmtops/Hand Held Devices

These PCs are small enough to be held in the palm of your hand. They use scaled-down versions of desktop software, e.g. Windows CE. One of the market leaders in palmtop computers over the past few years has been the PSION range – strictly speaking not a PC at all as it uses a different operating system and software.

Network computers

You can use your PC as a stand alone computer, or you can link it together with other computers to form a network. PCs can be networked in a simple *peer-to-peer* setup that allows peripherals, e.g. printers and scanners, to be shared. A user can also access files on another user's hard drive in this type of network.

Alternatively, PCs can be networked through a central computer (called a *server* or *file server*) where they can share drives and folders. Each user is allocated a specific area of hard drive on the server for their own data files. The file server also stores application software that can be run over the whole network, e.g. e-mail, anti-virus, etc. Back-up procedures are simplified for the user in this set-up as all files on the server can be backed up at the same time (often at night, when most people have gone home) rather than each user having to back-up the files from their own PC.

File servers are intended for business rather than personal use and they are more expensive than standard PCs.

Mainframe and minicomputers

Mainframes and minicomputers are much bigger than PCs (although PCs may be connected to them via a network). These computers are large file servers that store and process the data for a whole organization. Banks, insurance companies and retail stores, e.g. Boots, will often use mainframes. Smaller organizations may be able to get by using a minicomputer.

Data input terminals

These *look* like computers, but are actually input devices for the computer proper. You may have seen a data input terminal in action at the checkout of your local store where the barcode reader scans the item purchased and enters the data into the central computer. The central computer will process the data that has been entered via the data input terminal. The central computer may deal with stock control and re-ordering of goods as necessary. You will also encounter data input terminals at your bank and in the travel agents when you go to book your holiday – the terminal can be used to display information and enter details of bookings.

Some data input terminals have limited processing capabilities, and these terminals are called *intelligent* terminals. Terminals with no processing capabilities are called dumb terminals. ✓

Main parts of a PC

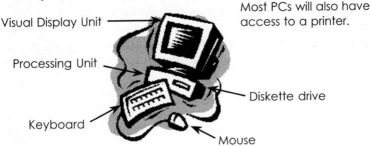

Visual Display Unit

Processing Unit

Keyboard

Diskette drive

Mouse

Most PCs will also have access to a printer.

Input devices

The **keyboard** is used to type information into your computer.

A **mouse** allows data input by selecting options (rather than typing in) – you click on the option required.

Output devices

Visual Display Unit (VDU): information that has been entered into the computer can be viewed on the VDU (also called a monitor).

VDU JARGON

Pixels: dots of light on the screen.

Resolution: the number of pixels on the screen. Generally speaking, the more pixels the better the picture. A resolution of 640 × 480 means that there are 640 pixels across and 480 down the screen. A resolution of 800 × 600 is also common.

Refresh rate (or scan rate): the frequency at which the dots of light flash on the screen. Typically, the refresh rate is 60 times per second.

The **size** of a VDU varies. The measurement quoted is for the diagonal measurement of the screen itself. Most PCs come with a 14" or 15" VDU as standard, with 17" monitors becoming standard on some systems (the more expensive ones). Prices are coming down and 17", 19" and 21" VDUs are becoming more affordable.

Printers

Printers are used to produce hard copy (printouts) of the data in your computer – text, pictures, graphs, etc. There are different types of printers, each with their own advantages and disadvantages. Inkjet printers are good in low volume situations, e.g. home use – they are fairly cheap to buy, but the ink cartridge is quite expensive.

Laser printers are better for business use where high quality high volume printing is needed. These printers are quite expensive to buy, but the running costs are less when high volume is required.

You may also come across a dot matrix printer – an older, noisier type – cheap, but not as popular as they once were.

Summary of printer types				
	How it works	Price	Running costs	Other info
Dot Matrix	Small pins are grouped together to form letters, the pins hit a ribbon giving the letter shape on the paper.	Cheap <£100	Cheap – ribbons last a long time.	Poor quality output. Noisy. Not used much except perhaps to print invoices, etc. Reasonably quick.
Ink Jet	Use an ink cartridge, giving a very fine spray to form the letters, etc.	Fairly cheap £80 – £100	Replacement cartridges relatively expensive – about £25.	Colour models give impressive results. Good for low-volume home use. Speed 3–12 ppm (pages per minute).
Laser	Create an electro-static image on a drum that picks up dry ink (toner) and transfers the image to the paper.	Expensive to buy: £400 – £3000	Low running costs per page printed.	Quicker than other types of printer – up to 24 ppm. Good investment for long-term, heavy use.

The processing unit

The processing unit (a desktop or tower, metal or plastic box) contains:

Electronics: e.g. the Central Processing Unit (CPU) and other microchips.

Hard disk drive: a storage device. Used for storing programs and data.

Floppy disk drive: allows a diskette to be used for storage. Facilitates the easy transfer of data (and programs) from one computer to another.

CD-ROM drive: reads information from a standard CD (similar to a music CD). The CD may contain music or applications software or data. Most applications are issued on CD.

Modem: allows the PC to connect to the telephone system and use e-mail and the Internet (some PCs have an *external* modem rather than an *internal* one).

Peripherals

Any piece of equipment attached to a PC rather than built into it is called a *peripheral* device. Printers, scanners, external drives, external modems, speakers, amplifiers, etc. are all peripheral devices. External devices can enhance the capabilities of your PC.

1.2   Hardware

Central Processing Unit (CPU)

The CPU is often referred to as the *brain* of the computer. It performs the core processing, logic control and calculation work on the information which is either input by the operator or specified by the software. It controls the information flow between secondary memory and main memory. A CPU constructed on a single chip is called a *microprocessor*.

The *clock speed* of the CPU is the speed at which it can process information. The clock speed is measured in megahertz (MHz). Mega = million, Hertz = cycles per second. A clock speed of 600 MHz therefore means that the processor can operate at 600 million cycles per second.

The clock speed of a computer is *one* of the factors that can influence its performance. Generally speaking, the higher the clock speed the more expensive the computer. Intel (with its Pentium and Celeron ranges) and AMD (with its K and Athlon series) are the main producers of processors.

Input devices

An input device is any device that enables you to enter data or give instructions to your computer. The ones that you are most likely to be familiar with are the keyboard and the mouse. Other input devices include:

Trackballs and **touchpads** are often found on laptops instead of a mouse. A trackball is like an upside-down mouse, and you use your fingertips to move the ball (which has the effect of moving the pointer on the screen). A touchpad senses a fingertip being drawn across it and moves the mouse pointer on the screen accordingly.

Scanners are used to convert printed material into a digitized form that can be imported into a computer application package. The scanner will take a 'picture' of the printed material, and the picture can then be stored or viewed on your PC. If you wish to scan in text and then manipulate it using a word processing application, you will need Optical Character Recognition (OCR) software. This software will convert the printed image into a form that can be used in a word processing application.

A **graphics tablet** is a touch sensitive pad that has a stylus attached to it. The stylus can be used to write or draw freehand onto the pad, and the data is converted into a digitized form that can be used in your computer.

In a **digital camera**, photographic images are stored in a digital format, directly onto magnetic media. The images can then be downloaded into your PC, and edited/printed and stored as required.

With **voice recognition**, a microphone is attached to a PC that has appropriate voice recognition software on it. When you speak into the microphone the speech is converted into text. The text can then be stored, edited and printed as required. This method of input could be very useful for visually or physically impaired PC users.

Joysticks are used to play games.

Output devices

An output device is any device that allows what is on your PC to be seen or heard. Output devices that you are likely to be most familiar with are the VDU and a printer (discussed above).

Other output devices include a plotter, speakers and speech synthesizers.

Plotters are a specialized type of printer used in design environments for things like technical drawings or architectural plans. They can print out large, complex hard copies. The computer software controls a type of pen that moves in two-dimensions over paper.

Speakers tend to come as standard on a *multimedia* PC, which is the type of PC often purchased for home use. They work in exactly the same way as speakers attached to your stereo equipment. Speakers on a PC may be self-powered, with a small amplifier built in. They usually require a soundcard to be fitted inside the computer and the speakers are then connected to this card.

Speech synthesizer software translates written text into audible speech. It has specialist uses, e.g. to help people with impaired vision or those with physical disabilities.

1.3   Storage

Disks

The units of measurement used to describe storage capacity on computers are bits, bytes, kilobytes, megabytes and gigabytes. The capacity of disks and memory size are measured in these units. As storage capacity is constantly increasing, the measurements most often used are megabytes (Mb) and gigabytes (Gb).

Hard disks contain your application software (word processing, spreadsheets, etc.) and your data.

A PC will usually be sold with a hard disk drive (HDD) built into it. However, you can buy additional HDDs to increase your storage space – you can get HDDs to fit inside your PC (an internal drive), or ones that plug into your PC but sit outside the unit as a *peripheral* (an external drive). External drives are more expensive than internal ones, and the cost of a

Unit of measurement	
1 bit	The amount of storage space needed to hold either a 1 or 0 in memory
1 byte	8 bits. Every character is made up of 8 bits (one byte), so each character takes up one byte of storage space
1 kilobyte (Kb)	1024 bytes. Double density diskettes have a capacity of 720 Kb.
1 megabyte (Mb) – about 1 million bytes	1024 kilobytes. PC Memory size is usually quoted in Mb. High density diskettes have a capacity of 1.44 Mb.
1 gigabyte (Gb) – 1 billion bytes	1024 megabytes. Hard disk sizes are usually quoted in Gb – on new PCs the hard disk will typically be about 10 Gb.

drive increases with its capacity. The capacity of HDDs is constantly increasing but typically they store from 6 Gb to 30 Gb.

The *access time* (the time taken for the unit to search for, identify and process data saved on the disk) of a HDD is measured in milliseconds (msec). In general, larger capacity HDDs tend to have a faster access time than smaller ones.

A **floppy disk** drive uses floppy disks (diskettes). Diskettes store less information than HDDs, high density diskettes having a capacity of 1.44 Mb. Other than capacity, the main difference between HDDs and diskettes is that diskettes are portable (unlike HDDs that are internal or plugged into your PC). Diskettes are often used to take backup copies of data files, in case the original file becomes corrupted (gets damaged). Diskettes are the cheapest type of storage media, but they are becoming less popular as higher capacity options become available at a reasonable price.

Iomega **Zip drives** have become increasingly popular in recent years. They combine the portability of a diskette with a higher capacity disk (originally 100 Mb, with 250 Mb disks now on the market). The zip drives use special zip disks, which look similar to, but a little bigger than, diskettes. Zip drives can be fitted internally or externally.

Compact disks (CD-ROM) have been used on PCs for several years. You can't store your data on a CD-ROM (Read Only Memory), but application packages are usually distributed on them. CD-ROMs used for PC application packages can store up to 650 Mb of information on them. They are ideally suited for storing information that doesn't need to be updated often, e.g. application packages (you buy the next version if you want to change it), encyclopaedias, e.g. Encarta, clipart, etc. In addition to storage capacity, increased speed of access is another benefit of CDs. ✓

CDs (like all other areas of IT) are continually developing. Recently developments have resulted in CDs that you can write to, in the same way as a HDD. There are two types of CDs that you can write to – CD-R (Recordable) and CD-RW (ReWriteable). With a CD-R you can use the disk to record information once only – once you've recorded something on it you can't re-record. With a CD-RW you can record, and re-record, as often as you want – the disks are reusable.

DVDs (Digital Versatile Disks) are beginning to supersede CDs. They have storage capacities of 4–5 Gb. You can store audio, video or computer program data on a DVD. CD-ROMs can be used in a DVD drive, but a DVD disk will not operate in a CD drive. DVD-R (recordable) is also available.

Advances in CD-ROM technology from the mid 1990s:

CD ➡ CD-R ➡ CD-RW ➡ DVD ➡ DVD-R

The storage devices discussed above are sometimes referred to as *secondary storage*.

Types of memory

Random Access Memory (RAM) is what is often referred to as *main memory*. The programs and data you are working on are stored in RAM. RAM is *volatile* memory – when the computer is switched off anything in RAM is lost. The CPU controls the flow of programs and data to and from RAM. Data that has been stored on disk is transferred into RAM when you open the file to work on it.

PCs will typically have between 16 Mb and 128 Mb of RAM – 128Mb is now common on higher specification PCs. Many new applications will not run satisfactorily on less than 16 Mb. It is possible to add more RAM if you wish.

Read Only Memory (ROM) is similar to RAM, but its contents are not lost when the computer is switched off. ROM is sometimes referred to as *secondary* memory. The CPU can read the contents of ROM, but can't add anything to it.

PC performance

A number of factors can affect a computer's performance – the speed at which it performs the tasks requested of it. You can judge a computer's performance in a number of ways – perhaps the amount of time it takes to open an application or file, or the amount of time it takes to display a graphic on the screen. Things that may affect the performance are:

* the clock speed of the CPU
* the amount of RAM
* the size of the HDD
* the access speed of the HDD
* the access speed of any peripheral device that the computer gets information from e.g. modem, external drives.

For a PC to operate at its optimum level, the capability of components has to be balanced. There is little point having 128 Mb of RAM and a 30 Gb HDD on a computer with a 133 MHz chip – the processor speed would not allow the optimum performance of the memory or HDD.

1.4   Software

There are two basic types of software that you should be aware of: operating system (OS) software and application package software.

Operating system

The OS is essential to the efficient running of the PC. It controls which operations within the computer are carried out and in what order they are done. It ensures that when you press a key on your keyboard, the instruction is translated into something the computer can work with.

When a computer is switched on it is said to *boot-up*. During the boot-up process, it carries out a Power On Self Test (POST) to check that the hardware components are present and working and to check that the CPU and memory are functioning correctly. The next thing that the computer does when it boots-up is to locate and load the OS (or part of the OS). The OS is usually stored on disk, e.g in your Windows folder. The OS is loaded into RAM at this stage.

The OS that you will become familiar with when working through this book is Microsoft Windows – you may be using Windows 95, Windows 98, Windows Me or Windows NT.

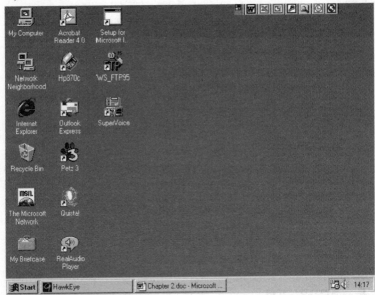

Windows has a Graphical User Interface (GUI) – it uses pictures (icons) to show the facilities available on the PC rather than words. You can select a feature by pointing to it with the mouse and then clicking on the feature you want to choose. Using a GUI as the front end to an OS makes it much easier for a user to tell the system what to do. Apple Macs also have a GUI.

Application packages

Computer programs like word processing, spreadsheet, database, etc. are called application packages. Application packages are separate from the OS, but they must be compatible with it. If you read the information on the box of an application package in a PC store, it will tell you what OS it is compatible with.

Popular application packages are:

Word Processing: used to produce reports, memos, letters, books – anything that is text based.

Spreadsheet: you can enter text and numbers into a spreadsheet, and, most importantly, perform calculations on the numbers and produce graphs.

Database: used to keep data on customers, suppliers, stock items, library books, etc. Data from a database can be *extracted* using different criteria, e.g. you might want a list of all the books in your library by a particular author.

Presentation: allows the creation of sophisticated presentations with text, pictures, graphs, video and music.

Desktop Publishing (DTP): useful for newsletters, posters, invitations, etc. where you want to have a lot of control over where you place your text and graphics on a page. Many of the more sophisticated word processors have similar capabilities to a DTP package.

Graphic Design: giving designers the opportunity to produce complex, detailed designs that can be edited and updated quickly and easily.

Accounts: used by companies to keep track of their cash flow.

Games: loads are available, there's something to suit every age group.

Many applications packages are sold as a *suite*, e.g. Microsoft Office or Microsoft Works. These contain sets of packages, e.g. word processing, spreadsheet, presentation, database, desk top publishing. Both Works and Office are popular suites found in the home and in all types of businesses. The applications in Office are much more powerful and sophisticated than those in Works making it more suited to business use.

Systems development

Most organizations use computerized systems. New systems are usually developed and introduced in the hope that the system will give the organization a competitive advantage over its rivals, e.g. make it more efficient so its prices can be kept low or its service improved. Introducing a new computerized system to an organization is no easy task. Many professionals are involved at the various stages as the system is developed and implemented.

A typical systems development cycle is described here, but there are other approaches.

Research

The first stage in the systems development cycle is to research the current system (if any) to establish what needs to be done, or to discuss the system requirements with those requesting it. This job is done by a *systems analyst*, who will talk to people in the organization and find out *exactly* what they do and why they do it. The systems analyst must get a very clear picture of what is required and why.

Analyze

The systems analyst will then analyze the information and start to plan the new system (which may be similar or very different to any existing one). It is important that the analyst incorporates all the information required into the new system and identifies what information will need to be extracted from the system.

At this stage the systems analyst will be able to help the organization identify:

*   hardware requirements
*   software requirements (it may be possible to buy something off the shelf, or special programs might need to be written)
*   networking requirements.

Program

If a program cannot be bought off the shelf one will have to be written to perform the tasks required. This job will be given to a *programmer*. The systems analyst will tell the programmer what the program must be able to do, and the programmer will write one to meet the specification given.

Test

Once the program has been written it must be tested. Test data is usually used for this (rather than live company data). Data will be entered and operations will be carried out on the data to check that the program works properly – calculations may be performed, reports produced, data extracted, etc. Any errors (bugs) detected will have to be fixed. The fixing of a program is often called *debugging*.

Implement

Once the software is working properly the new system can be implemented. The system will be distributed to all areas that will use it, training will be given, and the staff will start using the system.

Support

The system will need to be supported. There may be an individual or a help desk that can be contacted if things go wrong. The support given may be related to the hardware, software or to the users of the system.

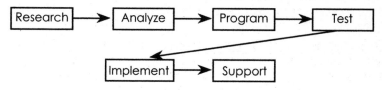

1.5 Information networks

Two or more computers connected together form a *network*. A network may consist a couple of computers in the same office sharing a printer and files or thousands of computers connected across the globe.

Local Area Network (LAN)

A LAN is made up of computers connected together by cables in the same room or building. The computers are in close proximity (local) to each other. Benefits of linking PCs together into a LAN are that several PCs can share the same peripherals, e.g. printer, scanner. The PCs can also share application and data files easily and they can communicate using e-mail (provided e-mail software is installed).

Wide Area Network (WAN)

Computers connected over a long distance are part of a WAN. Large organizations may use a WAN to connect their offices in different parts of the country. For example, an organization with branches in London, Leeds, Cardiff, Birmingham, Glasgow and Edinburgh may have the offices connected using a WAN (the computers at each branch would be connected

using a LAN). The WAN could typically have leased
lines from a phone company for the exclusive use of
the organization.

The advantages of linking PCs to a WAN is that
data can be transferred a long distance very quickly
(e.g. from the London office to the one in Edinburgh).

A computer linked to another via a modem over the telephone line would
be part of a WAN. Computers linked via the Internet form a WAN. A PC
attached to a WAN can have access to huge amounts of information (on
the Internet) and communicate with others using e-mail (which is much
quicker than sending information using the traditional mail service).

Modem (Modulator/Demodulator)

This device is used to link computers to the telephone line. It converts
(modulates) a digital signal from the computer into an analogue wave that
can be transmitted across the telephone network, then changes the signal
back from analogue to digital at the other end (demodulates). It is usually
fitted in the processor box. Modems work at a variety of speeds (the *baud
rate*) from 14,400 bps (bits per second) up to 56,600 bps. Although faster
modems cost more than slower ones there are potential savings to be made
on your line costs as the faster modems send and receive data much quicker.

Integrated Services Digital Network (ISDN) and Public
Switched Data Network (PSDN)

Instead of having a dedicated link between one LAN and another, i.e. a
WAN, it is possible to dial up digital connections as and when required.
These connections are called *circuit-switched digital services*. ISDN is an
example of this type of system. This type of telephone link is much faster
than the PSDN – the analogue network that you are probably connected to
when you use your telephone or PC from home. A digital network trans-
fers data much quicker than an analogue one, as there is no need for a
modem, and the data transferred is much less susceptible to corruption
(data getting lost, etc.).

Internet

The Internet is a WAN of sorts. Computers from all over the world are
linked together to form the Internet.

To access the Internet you need:

- a computer linked to the telephone network via a modem
- Internet software, e.g. Internet Explorer or Netscape Navigator
- an account with an Internet Service Provider (ISP). Your ISP will provide you with a connection to the Internet – usually at the same rate as a local phone call.

You can find about and learn how to use the Internet in Chapter 7.

World Wide Web (WWW)

The WWW is a vast collection of information stored on *web pages* and on *web sites*. Anyone connected to the Internet can view, read, print and/or download the information held on the WWW.

Search engine

The WWW contains a vast amount of information. To help users find the information they want on the WWW, a *search engine* can be used. There are several search engines to choose from e.g. AltaVista, Yahoo, Excite. You can locate the search engines at their web sites, e.g. www.yahoo.com. When using a search engine you enter the word or phrase you are looking for into a text field – the search engine then produces a list of web pages and sites that make reference to what you have searched for. Depending on how specific you have been in entering your request, and depending on the search engine used, you may have a few sites suggested – or hundreds or thousands!

Electronic mail (e-mail)

If you have access to the Internet you can send e-mail to anyone else that is connected. An e-mail is a message that is sent over a LAN or WAN. You can send text, data, pictures, etc. Messages received can be read, replied to, forwarded to someone else, stored, printed or deleted as required. Everyone that uses e-mail has a unique address. E-mail is very quick and cheap and compares very favourably with the traditional mail service.

You can learn how to use e-mail in Chapter 7.

1.6   Computers in everyday life

At home

Many homes have computers and the number is on the increase. Most home computers are *multimedia* systems that can be used for work and play. A multimedia system will be able to run application software, play music, playback video, run games software, and access the Internet, etc.

A computer at home has many uses:

*   Word processing software allows people to do letters, reports, invitations, lists, etc. on their PC. Spreadsheet software would mean that the home accounts could be prepared on the PC.

*   School pupils and students would find a home PC useful for homework and research. Encyclopedias are available on CD and access to the Internet gives access to information on any subject you care to mention.

*   Internet access on a home PC also means that you can do home banking (if your bank provides the facility).

*   Computer games are also popular on home PCs (games can also be played via the Internet).

*   Home shopping is on the increase – many high street retail outlets have web sites and specialist Internet retailers, e.g. Amazon.com, have emerged.

*   The number of people working from home has increased as many jobs that traditionally had to be done in the office can be carried out successfully on a PC at home. This *home working* is associated with the term SoHo (small office/home office). The benefits of home working are that it is flexible (you don't need to stick to the 9 to 5 routine), and you don't need to join the commuter trail to and from the office each day. However, some home workers feel isolated as they miss the social interaction of a central office.

At work/in education

Typical office applications software includes:

Word Processing for letters, reports, minutes, memos, etc.

Spreadsheet for budgets, sales figures, anything involving calculations.

Database for customer records, supplier information, product information, personnel records.

Presentation for meetings, lectures, conferences.

Information management for electronic diaries and organizers.

Accounts to keep tabs on purchases and sales.

Desktop publishing for company newsletters, leaflets.

In addition to the packages mentioned above, specialized businesses may use applications specific to their area of work, e.g. graphic design packages or photographic image manipulation packages.

Schools and colleges use in the classroom, applications such as Microsoft Works which are similar to those found in industry, to familiarize pupils with the type of software they will meet later in life. The administration requirements of educational establishments mean that the business applications found in the Office suite are usually required, e.g. database for student records, word processing for minutes/reports/teaching materials, etc.

In industry, computers are used to control production lines, control the manufacturing process and monitor stock control.

Computer Aided Design and Computer Aided Manufacturing (CAD/CAM) is a process where computer software is used to design components on screen. The same software then uses the design information to control the machine that manufactures the component.

Government agencies use computers to store NHS records, housing information, social security records, criminal records, etc.

Computers are particularly useful when:

- performing repetitive tasks
- doing fast and accurate calculations
- manipulating data
- extracting data from different sources.

There are times, however, when the human touch is better. Many people would rather speak to someone if they have a query than enter or extract data from a computer. People are also better at dealing with one-off situations – computers can't use their initiative or react to situations that they are not programmed to deal with – people can!

Computers in daily life

Computers play a large role in our daily life. Areas that you'll find them in include:

- **Bills**: gas, electricity, water, telephone, etc. are all computerized.
- **Money**: Automatic Teller Machines (ATMs), or debit and credit cards use computers to record transactions.
- **Medical records**: many doctors and dentists keep patient records on computer.
- **Supermarkets**: barcode readers identify the product bought and the price is located on computer, the stock records are adjusted to reflect the sale.
- **Library books**: many libraries use electronic tagging to facilitate computerized records of when books are issued and when they should be returned.
- **Smart cards**: cards with a microchip that contains a considerable amount of information about the holder could be used as combined debit/credit cards, identity cards, driving licence, emergency medical details, etc. Still relatively new, their use will most likely increase in the future.

1.7   IT and society

This section discusses some terms you may encounter as you read about developments in IT.

The term **Information Superhighway** is used to describe a situation where information of any kind, anywhere in the world, would be available to anyone who had access to a PC linked to the Internet. You can travel along the highway until you find what you are looking for.

The term **Information Society** may mean two things:

- A society where an increasing proportion of the working population is employed in collecting, processing, storing, retrieving and transferring information.
- A society where people have access to an almost unlimited amount of information via the Internet (in their homes or at work) without having to look it up in reference books or visit libraries.

The **millennium bug** (Y2K) was a potential problem for companies and their computers when the year became 2000. Many programs were written decades ago, and, as storage was very expensive, the date was represented by six characters – two for the day, two for the month and two for the year, e.g. 10/12/68 meant the 10th of December 1968. However, using this method, 10/12/00 would mean the 10th of December 1900 (which would be wrong in the vast majority of cases). Much work was needed.

Companies appointed Y2K project managers to oversee the work being done. The year part in the date fields had to be changed from two to four characters so that computer systems would recognize 1900 and 2000 dates correctly, or changes had to be made to the way that the programs interpreted the dates. Newer software written towards the end of the century that could cope with the year change was marketed as '2000 compliant'.

The press suggested many possible problems when 2000 arrived – banking systems failing, traffic management systems failing, etc. Much work was done to minimize the impact of the new millennium on our computer systems and as a result no serious mishaps were reported. The world as we know it did not end!

The Internet has facilitated the expansion of **e-commerce**. Companies can advertize their products on their own web sites on the Internet, take orders and accept payment via secure credit card transfer.

Electronic Data Interchange (EDI) refers to a situation where all communications in a business transaction are done electronically. An example would be computers in a retail environment. As items are purchased by the customer, details of the item are entered into the computer via the bar code reader at the checkout. This information automatically updates the stock records. When the stock levels reach the re-order level, an order would be raised and sent to the supplier electronically (using an EDI facility) and payment could be authorized at the same time. The supplier's computer would respond electronically to the order, arrange despatch of the goods and prepare and send the invoice.

Business people worldwide can have face-to-face meetings using **video conferencing**. Video cameras are linked via computers and the Internet so that people can see who they are talking to without leaving their office. A lot of time and money can be saved by holding meetings this way. People do not need to travel or pay expensive hotel bills.

A good workspace

It is important that the area you work in is comfortable and suitable for the type of work you are doing. Your working environment must conform to the relevant Health and Safety at Work (HASAW) legislation.

Things to consider when assessing whether or not the working environment is suitable for computer use include:

Lighting and ventilation, e.g.

- Provision of adequate lighting.
- Positioning of VDUs – the screens should not flicker or suffer from interference, and they should be free from glare.
- Provision of blinds if necessary to minimize the effect of direct sunlight on the VDU.
- Provision of adequate ventilation.

Operator comfort, e.g.

- Provision of movable keyboards.
- Suitable desktop space.
- There should be sufficient desk room and leg room to allow for posture changes.
- Provision of a document holder at a suitable height.
- An adjustable chair.
- Minimized printer noise (printer noise was a particular problem with dot matrix printers).

Safety, e.g.

- No trailing cables or power leads.
- No worn out or frayed power leads.
- No overloaded power points.
- No liquid near electrical components.

Problems that may be experienced by IT workers include:

- Backache and pains in general associated with bad posture and sitting in the same position for too long.
- Repetitive Strain Injury (RSI) – the result of poor ergonomics combined with repeat movements of the same joints over a long period of time.

- Eye strain – caused by flickering VDUs and not taking regular breaks from the PC screen (10 minutes every hour is recommended).
- Back injuries from lifting heavy objects, e.g. boxes of printer paper.
- Electric shocks due to dangerous wiring or poor working practice.
- Injuries resulting from tripping over trailing cables or other obstructions.

It is the employer's responsibility to ensure that appropriate provision is made available to provide a safe and comfortable working environment. The employee has a responsibility to make sure that he or she makes use of them and goes about their job in an appropriate manner.

1.8 Security, copyright and the law

Security

Your computer equipment and the data on it is a very important resource. It is therefore important that you look after it and take precautions to ensure that, should anything happen to it, you can recover from the situation.

Hardware can be protected through insurance policies – if a PC is stolen or damaged you can take precautions to ensure that you will be able to replace it. Your software will most probably have been installed from CD, and if it becomes corrupted in any way you should be able to reinstall it from your original disks (which should be kept in a safe place).

However, protecting your *data* needs a bit more thought. Threats to your data include:

- power cuts (where any unsaved data will be lost)
- serious hardware fault
- physical damage (perhaps as a result of flood or fire)
- infection by a computer virus
- theft or other malicious act.

Lost files on a home computer may cause some inconvenience, but on a business machine the effect of losing data could ruin an organization.

To minimize the effect of such incidents, you should *back up* the data on your HDD regularly. You may just back up important files to diskette or to a zip drive, CD-R or CD-RW, or you may back up the whole drive.

In a business situation, backups may be done every few hours, at the end of each day, weekly, etc. – it depends on the organization and how much the files change in a period of time. In many organizations, data is backed up overnight when most people aren't at work and the process is usually at least partially automated.

The set of media containing the backups is called the *backing store*. Ideally, the backing store should be in a different location to the computer that the original data is on – at least in a different room, ideally in a different building altogether.

All backup media should be kept in an environment that is thief proof and flood and fire proof. A safe or vault is often used. Ideally more than one set of backup media should be kept.

The storage devices for backing store need to be large enough to hold all the files that are considered crucial to the operation of the organization. Specialized storage devices such as tape-streaming machines can be used, or CD-R or multi-gigabyte HDDs may be used.

For a home PC user, diskettes, a zip drive, CD-R or CD-RW can be used for backing up your data. Exactly how often you back up will vary from individual to individual – but if you've just spent hours working a project on your PC, it's a good idea to back up the files before you finish work.

Write protecting

Write protect hole

To protect diskettes against you accidentally overwriting their contents, you can write protect them. If you look at a high density diskette, you will notice that the casing has two square holes through it. One of the holes has a sliding tab which you can move to open or close the hole. If both square holes are open, the disk is write protected (you can open files from it, but you can't save to it), if one square hole is open the disk is write enabled.

Password protection

When working in a networked environment, there are various levels of password protection available to help ensure that authorized users only can access the system and open and edit the files held on it.

User-level: password protection can be assigned at a user level (through the operating system) so that only authorized users can access the system. With this type of password protection, the computer will pause as it boots up and you need to enter your user identification and password before you can go any further.

Folders/directories: some folders on the file server will be shared so that several users may have access to them. To ensure that authorized users only access these folders, passwords may be used.

Files (on any PC, not just networked): if you have files on the system that you don't want other users to be able to view or edit, you may be able to password protect the individual files (most modern applications allow the user to password protect individual files).

By using the password protection features available, the following security features could be available on a networked PC:

- A password to access the system.
- A password to gain access to a shared folder on the network server.
- A password to access a file.
- A password to allow editing of a file.

Different users can have different levels of security clearance assigned to them, allowing different users access to different parts of the system and its files.

Screen savers (on any PC, not just networked): these are used to prevent the VDU from becoming damaged by a static image displayed on it for a long period of time. If you use a screen saver on your PC, you can enter a password as one of the screen saver options. When the screen saver is displayed, it will be necessary for the password to be entered before the system can be accessed again.

Computer viruses

A computer virus is a piece of software that has been written often with the specific purpose of causing havoc on computer systems. The software is called a virus because it has been programmed to spread through the system and on to other computer systems, just like an infectious virus spreads through the general population.

Some viruses are harmless, they do no serious damage to your system, but serve to remind you just how vulnerable your system may be. Others can have disasterous effects – deleting files, corrupting disks, etc.

No computer is immune to virus attack (although there aren't too many mainframe viruses), but some basic safety precautions can help limit the chances of infection:

- Install reliable anti-virus software on your computer, and update it regularly.

- Use anti-virus software to scan your system for viruses regularly.

- Use anti-virus software to scan any removable disks before you open files on them.

- Scan any files downloaded from the Internet before you open them – viruses are often transmitted in attachments to e-mails.

- Install only genuine software from reputable sources.

Copyright

Software copyright legislation is in place to give the authors and developers of software the same rights as authors of published written or musical works.

When you buy software, you don't actually purchase the package, but you purchase a licence that allows you to use the software.

With some licences you are permitted to install a copy of the software on one computer, and take a backup copy of the software for security purposes. With other licences you may be able to install two copies of the software, e.g. one on your office machine and one on your laptop or home PC. This option recognizes the fact that people often use the software in two locations. Instead of having to buy two copies of the software you can install it on two computers – but you should only be using one copy at a time (you can't be in two places at once).

In a business situation, where you perhaps have 50 users on a network, you can buy a licence that allows you to run the number of copies you require at any one time. This works out much cheaper than buying the same number of individual licences. The licence should cover the maximum number of users you expect to be using the software at any one time.

Shareware

Shareware software is obtained on a kind of sale-or-return basis. You can obtain the software free, use it for a limited period, e.g. 30 days, then if you decide that you want to continue to use the software you should forward that appropriate fee (typically £10–£30) and become a registered user. At the end of the evaluation period the software may have been programmed to stop working or it may flash messages telling you to pay up!

Sometimes the evaluation copy of a shareware package will be a scaled down version of the whole package. If you decide to pay up and register then the full package will be sent to you.

Freeware

Freeware is similar to shareware, but it doesn't cost anything. Freeware authors and developers often produce the software to solve a particular problem they have had, or just as a personal project/challenge. Once the software is written, they make it freely available to anyone else who thinks that they'll find it useful.

If you use shareware or freeware software, try to ensure that it comes from a reputable source or is recommended in PC magazines, etc. The software may not have been tested as thoroughly as commercial software and it may contain bugs or viruses. There is however some very good, useful and safe shareware and freeware software available – just be careful!

Data Protection Act

The Data Protection Act appeared in 1984 in the UK. It states that users of personal data relating to living, identifiable individuals which is automatically processed should be registered with the Data Protection Registrar. The users of the personal data should then adhere to The Codes of Practice and Data Protection Principles set out within the Act.

The Data Protection Principles

The rules that must be followed by all organizations keeping personal data on individuals are listed here.

The personal data must be:

- obtained lawfully
- held securely

- used only for the purpose stated to the Data Protection Registrar (or compatible purposes)
- adequate, relevant and not excessive in relation to the purpose for which it is held
- accurate and kept up to date
- deleted when it is not longer required
- available to individuals so that they can access and check the information that is held on them.

As most organizations (even small ones) hold personal data – on customers, employees, suppliers, patients, etc. – they must be registered with the Data Protection Registrar.

1.9 Mock test

Read *The tests* section in the Preface before you start. When you take your ECDL test you will be asked to type your answers into an Answer File (this will be provided on a disk by the test centre), which will look similar to the layout below. You will be asked to open the Answer File, type the answers into the spaces provided, save the file and print it.

You could create a file with a layout similar to that below for a practice run if you wish.

Answer File

Name/Candidate ID:	
1	
2	
3	
4	
5	
6	
7	
8	

Time yourself when you try the sample questions – no more than 45 minutes! No cheating – you have to do the real thing closed book (with no notes to help you!). You must score at least 18/30 to pass.

Sample questions

1. Give a brief explanation for the following: E-mail, Millennium bug. What does SoHo mean? What does GUI stand for? **(4 marks)**

2. The following items are either input or output devices: Scanner, VDU. Describe briefly the function of each device and indicate whether it is an input or output device. **(4 marks)**

3. What does RAM stand for? Give two characteristics of RAM. What does ROM stand for? Give two characteristics of ROM. **(4 marks)**

4. List six software application types which might be used in the office or home environment. **(4 marks)**

5. Give four situations where you might encounter computer-based systems in your everyday life. **(4 marks)**

6. Describe six implications of the Data Protection Act with respect to the individual and their personal data. **(4 marks)**

7. Explain the terms Hardware and Software. Give an example of each. **(3 marks)**

8. Give 3 examples of hazards at a computer workstation. **(3 marks)**

SUMMARY

This chapter has discussed:

✓ The physical make-up of a personal computer.

✓ Basic concepts of Information Technology (IT).

✓ Hardware.

✓ Different types of computer.

✓ Different parts of a computer.

✓ Software — operating systems and application packages.

✓ System development.

✓ Information networks.

✓ IT in society.

✓ Health and safety issues.

✓ System security.

✓ Copyright and data protection laws.

2 | USING THE COMPUTER AND MANAGING FILES

AIMS OF THIS CHAPTER

This chapter covers the topics that will be assessed in Module 2 of the ECDL. As you work through the chapter, experiment with the various features (it's the best way to learn how to use them) as they are introduced and discussed. Topics discussed are: how to start, stop and restart your computer, the desktop, formatting diskettes, the folder structure and how to manage your files, finding files, different file types and using the on-line help system. We will take a brief look at a basic word processing package and find out how to create, save and print a file from it. At the end of the chapter you will find a mock test so that you can try out your skills using questions similar to those that you will find in the actual assessment.

2.1 Start, stop and re-start your computer

Switching on the computer

The exact location of the switches on a PC varies from model to model. Have a look at your PC and try to find the switches. The switch on the main unit (the box containing the hard drive, CPU, modem, etc.) will probably be somewhere on the front of the unit. The switch (if it has one) for the VDU will most probably be on the front of the unit, but it may be up the side or even on the back.

❶ Ensure that your PC is plugged in and the power is switched on at the socket.

❷ Press the ON/OFF button on the main unit.

❸   Switch on the screen (if necessary – with some PCs the screen is left switched on and it goes on and off with the main unit).

❹   Sit back and wait for a few seconds while your computer comes to life.

Your computer will display the *desktop* (see 2.2) ready for you to tell it what you want to do next.

Shut down the computer

When you have finished working on your computer it is important that you shut it down properly. If you don't shut the computer down properly you may get error messages the next time you boot up (switch on).

To shut down your computer:

❶   Click the **Start** button on the Taskbar (see 2.2).

❷   Choose **Shut Down**.

❸   Select *Shut down the computer?*

❹   Click **Yes**.

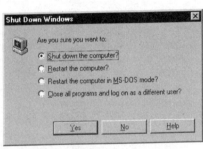

To re-start the computer

There may be times when your computer 'hangs' and refuses to do anything. When this happens it is impossible to shut it down in the normal way.

To restart the computer and recover from this situation:

❶   Press [Ctrl]-[Alt]-[Delete] on the keyboard simultaneously.

❷   At the **Close Program** dialog box, press [Ctrl]-[Alt]-[Delete] again.

◆   Your computer will restart.

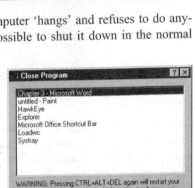

2.2 The Desktop

Your PC may be using Windows 95, 98, Me, NT or 2000. It doesn't matter which version of Windows is used, the Desktop will look similar on each.

- ♦ **Desktop** – the name given to the background area.

- ♦ **Icons** – the pictures on the desktop that provide shortcuts to applications, folders, files or other areas on your computer.

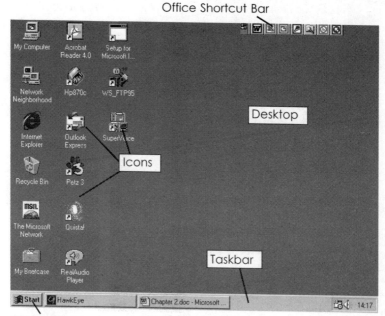

Office Shortcut Bar

Desktop

Icons

Taskbar

Start Button

- ♦ **Microsoft Office Shortcut Bar (MOS)** – a toolbar giving quick access to many of your applications. The location of this shortcut bar may vary – it could be top right (as in this screenshot), or along the bottom of the screen, or down the right or left side of the screen.

The tools on the MOS may also be different on your computer. The shortcut bar can be *customized* to display the tools you require.

- ♦ **Taskbar** – this is the bar displayed along the bottom of the screen. It contains the Start menu button. It will also display the names of any applications that are open and probably a clock (at the far right).

The Task Bar can also be customized, so the Task Bar on your machine may be slightly different from the example shown.

Some of the icons that appear on your desktop may be different to the ones in the illustration. For example, you may have:

 Double click this to see details of the drives and folders on your PC.

 Double click this to see what files have been deleted and are still available for recovery.

 A shortcut to an e-mail application.

♦ The icons can be moved around (provided the Auto Arrange option is switched off) – simply drag and drop them with the mouse.

To switch Auto Arrange on or off:

A tick indicates the option is switched on

❶ Right click anywhere on the Desktop.

❷ Click **Arrange Icons**.

❸ Click **Auto Arrange**.

♦ 'Click' means use the left mouse button, 'right click' will be used when you should click the right mouse button.

♦ When Auto Arrange is on, you can choose to arrange by Name, Type, Size or Date

Working with windows

When you view the drives and folders on your computer using My Computer or Windows Explorer, they are displayed in a window. When you open an application on your computer the application will be displayed in a window.

Let's have a look at a window using My Computer (don't worry if you don't understand everything that is displayed within the window, we're just looking at the basic structure of *all* windows).

❶ Double click on the Desktop. The My Computer window is opened.

It is important that you can recognize, name and know the purpose of the different parts of a window. The main areas are labelled on the diagram:

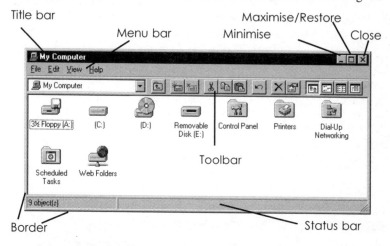

Maximize, minimize, restore

If a window is maximized it fills the whole screen – you cannot see any desktop area behind it.

If a window is not maximized, you will see some desktop area behind it.

♦   You can toggle between a window being maximized or not by clicking the **Maximize** and **Restore** buttons (or by double clicking the window Title Bar).

♦   A window can be minimized. Click the **Minimize** button.

The titles of all open windows are displayed on the Taskbar. (To move from one window to another, simply click on its title on the Taskbar).

♦   To restore a minimized window click on its name on the Taskbar.

Resize

If a window is not maximized you will be able to see its border. You can resize the window by dragging its border to make the window larger or smaller. The mouse pointer becomes a double-headed arrow when it is over a window border.

Move

Windows that are not maximized can be moved around the desktop. Drag the title bar of a window to move it.

Close

*   To close a window, click the **Close** ☒ button.

Look at some other windows and see if you can identify the different areas.

Try Windows Explorer:

❶   Open the **Start** menu.

❷   Select **Programs**.

❸   Click **Windows Explorer**.

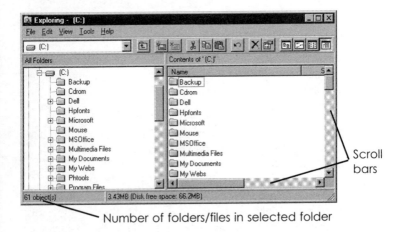

Number of folders/files in selected folder

You should be able to identify the different areas described earlier.

Some windows have *scroll bars* on them. You use the scroll bars to move up and down (or right and left) to display more information.

You could also have a look at WordPad (**Start ⇨ Programs ⇨ Accessories ⇨ WordPad**), Paint (**Start ⇨ Programs ⇨ Accessories ⇨ Paint**) or Solitaire (**Start ⇨ Programs ⇨ Accessories ⇨ Games ⇨ Solitaire**) and identify the different areas in the window.

If you have several windows open you can easily move from one window to another. Either:

❶ Click on the title of the target window on the Taskbar.

Or

❷ Hold down the [Alt] key and press [Tab].

◆ Keep the [Alt] key held down and press [Tab] repeatedly. You will cycle through the open windows. When the one you require is displayed on the screen, release the keys.

Shortcuts

You can create shortcuts on the desktop that take you to any folder or application on your system. To create a shortcut:

❶ Locate the folder or application that you wish to create a shortcut to (either in Windows Explorer or through My Computer).

❷ Restore/resize the window if necessary – so that you can see your desktop as well as the window.

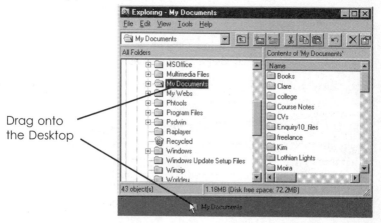

Drag onto
the Desktop

❸ Right click on the folder and drag it onto the Desktop.

❹ Release the mouse button.

❺ At the shortcut menu click **Create Shortcut(s) Here**.

◆ The shortcut will appear on your Desktop.

2.3   Menu bar

At the top of the My Computer and Windows Explorer window is the
Menu bar. You can use the Menu bar to access every command available
in that application. You can display a menu list and select menu options
using either the mouse or the keyboard.

Using the mouse

❶   Click on the menu name to display the list of op-
     tions available in that menu.

❷   Click on the menu item you wish to use.

Using the keyboard

♦   Hold down the [Alt] key and press the underlined letter in the menu
     name e.g. [Alt]-[F] for the File menu, [Alt]-[V] for the View menu.

To select an item from the menu list either:

♦   Keep the [Alt] key held down and press the underlined letter in the
     option required, e.g. O in the File menu to Open.

Or

♦   Use the up and down arrow keys on your keyboard until the item
     you want is selected, then press the [Enter] key.

Once a menu list is displayed, you can press the right or left arrow keys to
move from one menu to another.

To close a menu without selecting an item from the list:

♦   Click the menu name again, or click anywhere off the menu list or
     press the [Esc] key on your keyboard.

In addition to the menus, many of the commands can be initiated using the
toolbars or keyboard shortcuts.

2.4   Know your PC

System information

Most likely, your computer will consist of:

♦   a unit that holds the Central Processing Unit, memory, modem, a
     hard disk (C: drive), a CD or DVD drive and a 3 ½" diskette drive

- a keyboard
- a mouse
- a visual display unit (VDU)
- a printer
- and probably speakers so you can listen to your favourite music while you work!

Do you know anything about the specification of the computer that you are using? If someone asked you how much RAM your computer had or what processor it used would you be able to tell them?

If you need this information, you can easily find it in the System Properties dialog box. To access System Properties:

❶ Open the **Start** menu.

❷ Select **Settings.**

❸ Click **Control Panel**.

❹ Double click 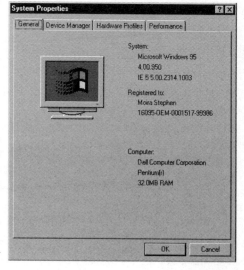.

The **System Properties** dialog box will appear. The **General** tab contains basic system information about your PC.

A *dialog box* looks similar to a window, but you should be able to spot a couple of basic differences.

- A dialog box has no minimize, maximize/restore buttons – you can't change the size of a dialog box (but you can move it by dragging its title bar).

- A dialog box has **OK** and **Cancel** buttons. If you make changes to the information that is in a dialog box, clicking **OK** will close the dialog box and make the changes take effect. If you click **Cancel**, the dialog box will close, but no changes will take effect.

In this example, the details regarding the computer's operating system, processor and RAM are:

+ Windows 95
+ Pentium Processor
+ 32 MB RAM.

Have a look at the other tabs in the dialog box – don't change anything!

Date & Time

At the far right of our Taskbar you will notice the clock [14:52   ]. If you move your mouse pointer over the clock, the current date will appear. You can switch the clock display on or off depending on your preference.

❶ Open the **Start** menu.

❷ Choose **Settings**.

❸ Click **Taskbar**.

❹ On the **Taskbar Options** tab, select the **Show Clock** checkbox.

❺ Click **OK**.

The date and time displayed on your clock should be accurate. If it isn't you can adjust the settings.

❶ Open the **Start** menu, choose **Settings** and click **Control Panel**.

❷ Double click 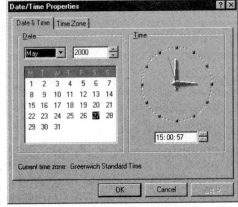 .

At the **Date/Time Proper-ties** dialog box, edit the set-tings as necessary

On the **Date & Time** tab, to set the date:

❶ Select a month from the drop-down list.

❷ Set the year (either use the split arrows to the right of the field, or select the current entry and type in the one required).

❸ Click on the correct date.

To set the time:

❶   Double click on the part of the time field that you wish to change – the hours, minutes or seconds.

❷   Use the split arrows to the right of the field to increase or decrease the value, or type in the value required.

On the **Time Zone** tab, to change the time zone:

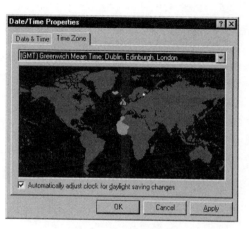

❶   Choose the time zone required from the drop-down list.

♦   Tick the **Automatically adjust clock** checkbox if you want to have your clock changed for you each spring/autumn.

❷   Click **OK**.

Volume settings

The volume settings used by your audio equipment may be controlled physically (by adjusting the volume on your hardware) or it may be possible to control the volume using software.

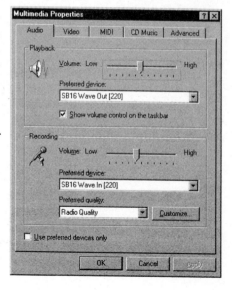

You can adjust the volume of the audio warning sounds (e.g. the sound you hear when you try to close a file without saving it) in Windows from the Control Panel.

❶   Open the **Start** menu, choose **Settings** and click **Control Panel**.

❷   Double click 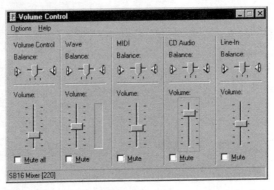 .
      Multimedia

❸   Adjust the **Playback** setting as required.

◆   Tick the **Show volume control on the taskbar** checkbox if you
      want it displayed.

❹   Click **OK**.

To change the volume of audio devices on your computer:

❶   Double click the **Volume Control** button ◀ on the Taskbar.

❷   Increase or decrease the volume of the required device.

❸   Click ✖ to close the dialog box.

Background display

The desktop on your computer can be customized in a variety of ways.
For example, you can select a background design for your desktop from a
list of *patterns* or *wallpapers*.

To choose a background:

❶   Open the **Start** menu, choose **Settings** and click **Control Panel**.

❷   Double click .
      Display

❸   Select the **Background** tab.

❹   Choose the pattern from the **Pattern** list or a wallpaper from the
      Wallpaper list.

❺ Select the display option required – to cover the whole desktop with the pattern or wallpaper or to affect a small area in the centre of the desktop.

Screen settings

If you need to change the screen settings for your PC (you may want to be able to see more on your screen or change the colour set) you can do so in the **Display Properties** dialog box.

To change the colour palette:

❶ Select the **Settings** tab.

❷ Select the colour palette required from the list.

❸ Click **OK**.

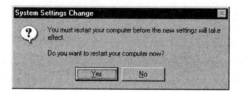

◆ You will be prompted to restart the computer for your change to take effect.

❹ Click **Yes** to get your new setting to take effect.

To change the resolution:

❶ Select the **Settings** tab.

❷ Drag the Desktop area slide control to the required position.

❸ Click **OK**.

Colour

When Windows is installed on a computer the default colour scheme is used for the desktop, active title bar, inactive title bar, etc. If you do not like the default colours, or if you wish to try something different, you'll find a number of colour schemes to choose from in the **Display Properties** dialog box.

❶ Select the **Appearance** tab in the **Display Properties** dialog box.

❷ Select a colour scheme from the **Scheme** list.

❸ Click **OK**.

Alternatively, you can create a custom colour scheme by changing the colour of individual areas found on the desktop and then save your colour scheme.

❶ Select the item you wish to set a colour for in the **Item** list.

❷ Set the colour required in the **Color** field.

♦ Some objects, e.g. Title Bar, also allow for the specification of font formatting for the text in the object. If you wish to change the font formatting do so using the Font, Size and Color fields and the Bold and Italic buttons (these options are inactive for any object that doesn't have text on it).

❸ Repeat steps 1 and 2 until you've customized the areas as you wish.

❹ Click the **Save As...** button.

❺ Give your colour scheme a name.

❻ Click **OK**.

♦ If you decide that you prefer the default colours, choose *Windows Standard* from the **Scheme** list to get back to the original settings.

Screen Saver

Screen savers are designed to protect your screen from the damage that can occur if it has a static image on it for prolonged periods. A screen saver is either a moving image or a blank screen that limits the damage that can be done to your screen. You should specify a screen saver for your PC. You'll find you've several to choose from, and they can be customized in a number of ways.

❶ Select the **Screen Saver** tab.

❷ Select a screen saver.

❸ Click **Settings** and customize the settings as required.

❹ Click **Preview...** to see how your screen saver looks.

❺ Repeat steps 2–4 until you are satisfied with your choice.

❻ If you wish to password protect your screen saver select the **Password protected** checkbox.

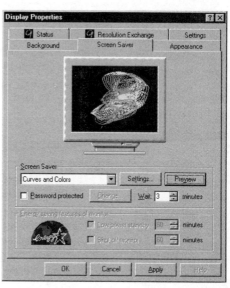

❼ Click the **Change** button, complete the **Change Password** dialog box as required and click **OK**.

❽ Set the **Wait time** (the length of time that the screen is inactive before the screen saver cuts in) – something between two and four minutes is usually fine.

❾ Click **OK**.

◆ Once the screen saver is set, it will appear on your screen any time that the PC is inactive for the time specified in the Wait field on the Screen Saver tab.

◆ When you move your mouse or press a key on your keyboard the screen saver will disappear and your work will be displayed again.

◆   If you set a password for your screen saver you will have to enter
     the password into a dialog box before you are allowed to access
     your work again. DON'T FORGET THE PASSWORD!

If you have set a password then decide you wish to switch the facility off,
return to the **Screen Saver** tab in the **Display Properties** dialog box and
deselect the *Password protected* checkbox.

2.5   Formatting diskettes

Most of the time that you work on a PC you will probably save your work
to the hard drive (C:) or to a network drive (H, J, Y, etc.). There may be
times, however, when you need to use a diskette, e.g.

◆   in a school or college situation where you do not have storage space
     allocated to you on the hard drive or network drive

◆   to move information from one PC to another

◆   to take a copy of some data files for security purposes.

If you are going to use diskettes, they must be formatted before you can
store information on them. You can buy boxes of disks that are pre-formatted (so they are ready to use), but not all diskettes are pre-formatted so
you must know how to format them.

You can also format diskettes that have already been used. Diskettes that
have been around for some time and have had a lot of use will benefit
from a re-format. When you format diskettes that contain data the data is
erased (so be careful that you don't format a diskette that contains something that you want to keep).

To format a diskette:

❶   Insert the diskette into the diskette
     drive (A:) on your PC (metal part
     goes in first, label facing upwards).

❷   Double click My Computer on the
     Desktop.

❸   Right click on the **3 ½" Floppy
     (A:)** icon and select **Format…**

❹   Select the disk **Capacity**. The de-
     fault (1.44Mb) is used for high

density (HD) diskettes (the most common type). If you are using double density (DD) diskettes set the disk capacity to 720Kb.

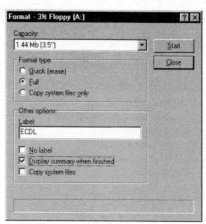

❺ Specify the **Format type**. If the diskette hasn't been formatted before this must be set to *Full*. If the diskette is being reformatted you can choose *Quick (erase)*.

◆ You can give your diskette a label (name) if you wish – maximum of 11 characters permitted.

❻ Select the **Display Summary** checkbox. The summary information is displayed once the formatting is complete. It tells you if any errors were encountered during formatting. If a diskette has errors on it when it's formatted – bin it! If you've just bought a new box of diskettes and several are faulty take them back to the shop.

❼ Click **Start** and sit back and wait while your diskette is formatted.

◆ When the formatting process is complete (it only takes a couple of minutes) the summary information is displayed. If your diskette has no errors on it the *total disk space* and *available disk space* figures should be the same. If there are faulty areas on the diskette they will be indicated in the *bad sectors* figure.

❽ Click the **Close** button on the **Format Results** dialog box.

◆ If you wish to format another diskette, remove the one you've just formatted, insert another diskette and repeat the process.

❾ When you've finished formatting your diskettes click the **Close** button in the **Format** dialog box.

2.6 Windows Help

It is important that you learn to find your way around the Help system – in Windows and also in any applications that you use. We will look at the Windows Help system here. Once you are familiar with one Help system you will very quickly find your way around any other.

To access the Windows Help system:

❶ Open the **Start** menu and choose **Help**.

The **Help Topics** dialog box is displayed.

You can interrogate the system through the Contents, Index or Find tabs.

Contents tab

The best way to have a browse through the Help is from the **Contents** tab.

The Help topics are grouped into books. You can open any book to view its contents by double clicking on it.

To return to the **Help Topics** dialog box, click Help Topics at the top of any Help page.

Sometimes a book will contain other books, sometimes it will contain the names of Help pages.

+ To display the contents of a page simply double click on it.

Spend some time exploring the Help system from the Contents tab.

Index tab

If you know the word or topic that you want help on, you can use the Index tab.

❶ Type in the first few letters in the first field on the Index tab.

+ The list of topics in the lower part of the dialog box will scroll to bring topics you may be interested in into view.

❷ Double click on the topic you want help on.

Or

❸ Click on the topic you want help on.

❹ Click **Display**.

+ You may be presented with another list of topics to choose from – just double click on the one you want.

❺ The Help page will be displayed.

Find tab

The third option is to use the Find tab.

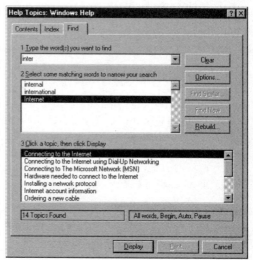

❶ Start typing the word(s) you want in the first field.

❷ Select a matching word from the list of words in the middle of the dialog box to narrow your search.

❸ Double click on the topic in the lower list that you are interested in.

Or

❹ Select a topic and click **Display**.

Glossary items

Some help pages contain glossary items –
green text with a broken underline. These
glossary items are jargon or technical terms
that you might not understand. You can get
a brief description of the term by clicking
on the word or phrase in the Help window.

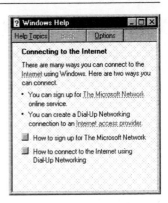

Retracing your steps

If you've moved through several Help pages, then decide that the information that you really needed was back a page or two, click [Back] until
you get back to the page required.

Printing a Help topic

If you want to print a Help topic out:

❶ Click [Options] at the top of the page.

❷ Choose **Print Topic...** from the list.

❸ Click **OK** at the Print dialog box.

♦ Explore the Help system. You may not understand some of the topics discussed in it, but try to get a feel for how it works and how
you can move around within it.

2.7 Organizing files

The programs and data that are stored on your PC are stored on disks
which are housed in drives. The drives are named using letters of the al-
phabet. Your diskettes use the A: drive. Your local hard drive is the C:
drive. Your CD-ROM drive is probably your D: drive. You may have other
drives, e.g. Zip drives for backups or network drives available to you.
They will be named E: F: G: H: etc.

We have already seen that you can display the contents of your computer
system and disks either through My Computer or by opening Windows
Explorer.

The structure of drives and folders is very hierarchical. The drives are displayed in My Computer, each drive identified by a letter (A:, C:, E:, etc.). If you display the contents of a drive you will find folders and files. Some of the folders will have sub-folders, and some sub-folders will have sub-folders (folders and sub-folders are sometimes called directories and sub-directories). The way that you organize the folders for your *data* files is up to you.

♦ The organization of folders that contain applications and system software should not be touched.

Creating folders

You should give careful consideration to the folder structure you use for storing your data.

If you are using Microsoft Office, the default location for your data files is the folder called My Documents.

You may be using a different folder for your default folder – perhaps one named after you, e.g. Moira's Work.

You can easily create additional folders to help you organize the data that you will create.

You can create a folder at the Drive level – immediately under the drive icon C: or A: etc, or you can create a folder within an existing folder.

Let's say I decided to create a folder on the C: drive for my work. Within my work folder, I want to set up a folder for the different areas of my work. The structure that I want to set up on the C: drive is:

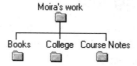

This structure could be created and modified in either My Computer or Windows Explorer.

My Computer

♦ Double click on the My Computer icon on the desktop to see what drives you have access to. In the example here I have access to an A:, C:, D: and E: drive.

Views   Small icons   List

Large icons   Details

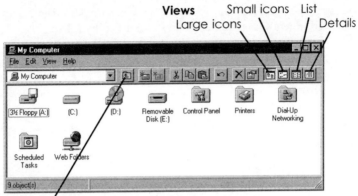

Takes you up to the previous level in the structure
if you've moved down through the folders

To view the contents of a drive or folder:

* Double click on the drive or folder.

To create a folder under the C: drive:

❶ Double click on the C: drive to view its contents.

❷ Open the **File** menu.

❸ Choose **New**, then **Folder**. A new folder will appear in the window

❹ Type in the name you want the folder to have, e.g. Moira's work,
(to replace the New Folder name).

❺ Press [Enter].

To create a folder within this new folder:

❶   Double click on the folder to open it then repeat steps 2–5 above.

To display the folder or file attributes, e.g. name, size, last updated, etc.:

♦   Click the **Details** view tool at the right of the My Computer toolbar.

To rename a folder:

❶   Select the folder.

❷   Open the **File** menu.

❸   Choose **Rename**.

❹   Type in the new name for the folder.

You can rename a file in exactly the same way – simply select the file name at step 1.

Windows Explorer

❶   Open the **Start** menu.

❷   Select **Programs**.

❸   Click **Windows Explorer**.

You can collapse or expand the view you have of your computer system in the pane on the left side of the window.

Selected drive or folder   View Icons

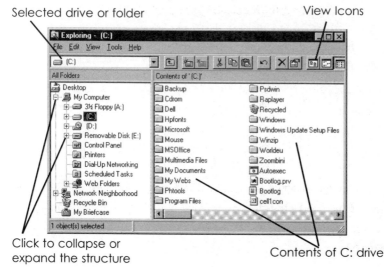

Click to collapse or
expand the structure   Contents of C: drive

♦   Click the + icon beside a drive, folder or My Computer to expand it and view the contents in the pane on the left.

♦   Click the - icon (displayed when a drive, folder or My Computer is expanded) to collapse the view in the left pane.

♦   If you click on a drive in the left pane, the contents of the drive will be displayed in the right pane of the window. The folders are displayed first, then the files.

♦   You can change the way the contents of a drive or folder are displayed by using the View icons on the toolbar.

To create a folder on the C: drive:

❶   Select the C: drive in the left pane of the Exploring window (it doesn't matter if the drive structure has been expanded or not).

❷   Open the **File** menu.

❸   Choose **New**, then **Folder**.

❹   A new folder will appear in the right pane of the window ▨ New Folder .

❺   Type in the name you want the folder to have, e.g. Moira's work (to replace the New Folder name) and press [Enter].

To create a folder within this new folder:

❶   Display the folder in the left pane of the Exploring window (expand the C: drive if necessary).

❷   Select the folder that you wish to create a new folder within (in the left pane of the Exploring window).

❸   Repeat steps 2–5 above.

Repeat as necessary until you have set up the structure you require.

To view the contents of a folder:

♦   In the left pane of the Exploring window, select the folder you wish to view the contents of. The contents will be displayed on the right pane of the window.

To display the folder or file attributes, e.g. name, size, last updated, etc.

♦   Click the **Details** tool at the right of the Exploring toolbar.

To rename a file or folder, use the same technique as in My Computer (page 53).

File types

Different file types are created by different applications. You can tell by the extension (the last three characters in a file name) what application or type of application the file was created in.

Extension	Application	File type
mdb	Access	Database
doc	Word	Word Processing
xls	Excel	Spreadsheet
bmp	Paint	Image file
pub	Publisher	Desktop Publishing
ppt	PowerPoint	Presentation graphics
htm	Various	Web page
rtf	Various	Word Processing

Copy, move and delete files and folders

If you wish to copy, move or delete a file or folder the first thing that you must do is *select* it.

To select an individual file or folder, click on it.

To select a group of adjacent files:

❶ Click on the first file or folder.

❷ Hold the [Shift] key down.

❸ Click on the last file or folder.

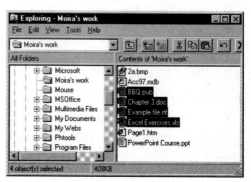

To select non-adjacent files:

❶ Click on the first file or folder.

❷ Hold the [Ctrl] key down.

❸ Click on each of the other files or folders as required.

To copy a folder or file(s):

❶ Select the folder or file(s).

❷ Open the **Edit** menu and choose **Copy**.

❸ Select the folder or drive you wish to copy the folder or file(s) into.

❹ Open the **Edit** menu and choose **Paste**.

To move a folder or file(s):

❶ Select the folder or file(s).

❷ Open the **Edit** menu and choose **Cut**.

❸ Select the folder or drive you wish to copy the folder or file(s) into.

❹ Open the **Edit** menu and choose **Paste**.

To copy or move a folder or file(s) onto a diskette:

❶ Select the folder or file(s).

❷ Open the **Edit** menu and choose **Copy** or **Cut** (depending on whether you wish to copy or move the folder or file(s)).

❸ Select the diskette drive.

❹ Open the **Edit** menu and choose **Paste**.

To delete a folder or file(s):

❶ Select the folder or file(s).

❷ Press [Delete] on your keyboard.

❸ At the Confirm folder or file prompt click **Yes**.

Deleted files and folders are placed in an area called the *Recycle Bin*.

Recycle Bin

If you accidentally delete a file you can restore it, provided it is still in the Recycle Bin. This can be opened from the Desktop or Windows Explorer.

To open the Recycle Bin:

- ◆ Double click on it on the Desktop, or select it in the left pane of the Exploring window.

To recover files that have been placed in the Recycle Bin:

- ❶ Select the file(s).
- ❷ Open the **File** menu and choose **Restore**. The files will be returned to their original folders.

To empty the Recycle Bin:

- ❶ Open the **File** menu.
- ❷ Choose **Empty Recycle Bin**.
- ❸ Click **Yes** at the prompt.
- ◆ Close the Recycle Bin, or select a different drive or folder.

Searching for folders or files

If you have forgotten which folder you put your file into, you should be able to find it using the Find command in Windows Explorer:

- ❶ Open the **Tools** menu.
- ❷ Choose **Find**, then **Files or Folders**.

To search for a file or folder using its name.

- ❸ Select the **Name & Location** tab.
- ❹ Type in the name (or part of the name if you don't know it all).

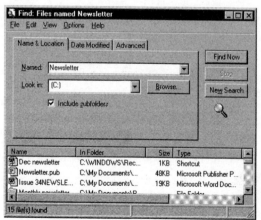

❺ Select the **Drive** that you want searched (or click **Browse** and locate the drive and/or folder you want to search from).

❻ Select or deselect the **Include subfolders** checkbox as required.

❼ Click **Find Now**.

A list of files or folders that match your search criteria will be displayed.

To search for a file using date criteria:

❶ Select the **Date Modified** tab.

❷ Specify the date option required.

❸ Click **Find Now**.

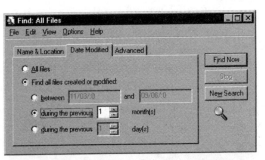

To search by file type:

❶ Select the **Advanced** tab.

❷ Choose the **File Type** required in the **Of type** list.

❸ Complete the **Containing text:** field as required.

❹ Specify the size (if known).

❺ Click **Find Now**.

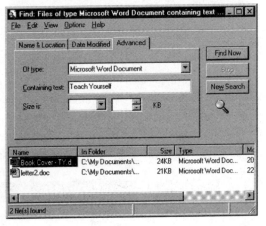

You can specify your search criteria on any combination of the tabs before you click **Find Now**.

Once you've found the file that you're looking for, double click on it in the Name list in the Find dialog box to open it.

2.8 Printing

Default printer

Your computer system may be set up so that you can print your files to one of several different printers – a laser, an inkjet, etc. When you print a file from an application it uses the *default* printer – the printer that has been set up as the one that you normally print to. You can change the default printer if you wish. The printer that you want to become the default must be installed before you do this procedure.

❶ Open **Start** menu.

❷ Point to **Settings**.

❸ Click **Printers**.

❹ Right click the icon for the printer you want to use as the default.

❺ Click **Set As Default** on the shortcut menu.

◆ If the option has a tick beside it, the printer has already been set as the default printer.

To view a print job's progress

If you have several files sent to print, you may want to check on the progress of your files. You can display a list of files that are waiting to print.

◆ Double click the Print icon ▓ on the right of the taskbar (displayed when there are documents in the print queue).

The window displays details of the jobs in the print queue.

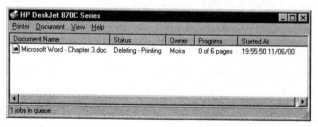

You can use the menus in the print queue window to pause printing, purge print jobs (empty the queue), etc.

2.9 Using a text editing application

The most commonly used application is probably word processing, such as Word or WordPad. Here we will take a brief look at a basic word processor called WordPad. This is part of Windows. (For Word see Chapter 3.)

To open and close WordPad:

♦   See *Opening and closing an application* in 8.1 (WordPad is in Accessories).

When you open WordPad, a new file is automatically created, and all you need to do to produce your letter or report is start typing. Your text will appear at the insertion point – the flashing black vertical bar in the document area.

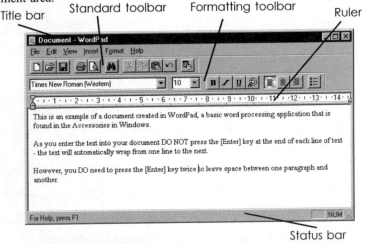

Title bar   Standard toolbar   Formatting toolbar   Ruler

Status bar

To save your file:

♦   See *File handling* (8.3).

To preview and print your document:

♦   See *Preview and Print* (8.11) – this includes notes on print to file.

To create a new document:

❶   Click the **New** tool on the Standard toolbar.

❷   Select the New Document type required, e.g. Word 6 Document.

❸   Click **OK**.

2.10 Mock test

Read *The tests* section in the Preface before you start. When you take your ECDL test you will be asked to type your answers into an Answer File (provided on a disk by the test centre), which will look similar to the answer file layout below. You could create a file with a layout similar to that below for a practice run if you wish.

In the ECDL test some of the folders and files will already have been set up on the disk provided by the test centre. For practice, you could use your own folders and files to check that you can perform the tasks required (see checklist below).

Answer File

Name:	
1	
2	
3	
4	
5	
6	
7	
8	
9	
10	
11	
12	
13	
14	
15	

Checklist

In the test, you will be provided with a disk that has some folders and files set up on it. You will be asked to perform a series of tasks on the folders and files on the disk to demonstrate your system management abilities.

At the end of the test the disk will be checked by the tester to ensure that you have followed the instructions correctly.

The tasks set will test your ability to:

◆   Create a folder structure (folders and subfolders)

◆   Count the number of files and folders within an existing folder (or folder structure)

◆   Count the number files of a given type e.g. .doc .rtf .xls within an existing folder (or folder structure)

◆   Copy files and folders

◆   Re-name files and folders

◆   Delete files and folders

◆   Restore files and folders.

For a practice run, time yourself 45 minutes and try the following list of tasks using your own files and folders:

◆   *Set up three folders in a simple folder structure (parent and two children)*

◆   *Rename a file and a folder*

◆   *Delete two files*

◆   *Move two files*

◆   *Copy two files*

◆   *Count the number of files in a folder*

◆   *Carry out the sample instructions and answer the sample questions.*

Sample instructions and questions

In addition to the above assessment tasks you will be asked a number of questions on the module content. The answers should be typed into the Answer File provided by the test centre. Below are sample instructions and questions which are similar to those you can expect in the ECDL test.

1. Open the *Answer File* from your disk. Type your name in the space provided at the top of the page. Save your *Answer File.*

2. What is the correct procedure for turning off a standard PC? Type clear instructions on how to do this into the *Answer File* and save it.

3. Which of the following key combinations will move you through your open files or applications? Enter your answer (1, 2, 3 or 4) in to the *Answer File* and save it.

   1 Esc+Enter   2 Alt+Tab   3 Shift+Enter   4 Ctrl+Alt+Delete

4. Use the Help Function to find information about 'Using Backup to back up your files'. Enter two lines of text information about 'Using Backup to back up your files' as your answer into your *Answer File* and save it.

5. Which of the following buttons should you click on to minimize a desktop window? Enter your answer (1, 2, 3 or 4) into your *Answer File* and save it.

   1 ▣   2 ☒   3 ▤   4 ▱

6. Which file type below is often used for database files? Enter your answer in the *Answer File* and save the *Answer File.*

   1 .mdb   2 .xls   3 .doc   4 .jpeg

7. Describe how to select another printer as the default printer from an installed printer list. Enter your answer in *Answer File* and save the *Answer File.*

8. Print two copies of the *Answer File* to a printer if available. If a printer isn't available save the *Answer File* as a print file.

SUMMARY

This chapter has discussed using the computer and managing files. You have found out about:

✓ Starting, stopping and re-starting your computer.

✓ The desktop and working with windows.

✓ Menus.

✓ Knowing your PC – system information, date & time, volume settings, background, screen settings and colours, screen savers, etc.

✓ Formatting diskettes.

✓ On-line Help.

✓ Creating and managing folders.

✓ Copying, moving and deleting folders and files.

✓ Printing – default printer and checking progress of print jobs.

✓ Using a basic text editing application.

3 | WORD PROCESSING

AIMS OF THIS CHAPTER

This chapter discusses features that are specific to Word (features common to all applications are discussed in Chapter 8 – make sure you go through them and can apply them in Word). Other topics include view options, indents, tabs, headers, footers, page numbering, tabs, numbered and bulleted lists, templates, styles, tables, mail merge and importing data from other applications. Experiment with the topics covered in the chapter – you have to do it to learn it. Remember to use UNDO (see 8.10) if you try something out and it doesn't go as expected!

3.1 Starting Word

When you start Word (see 8.1), a new blank document is displayed on the screen. Take a look at the Word screen – you should be able to recognize:

- Title Bar
- Menu Bar
- Toolbars
- Document area
- Border
- Status Bar
- Scroll bars
- Rulers
- Minimize, Maximize/Restore and Close buttons

The document name, *Document1*, is displayed on the document title bar.

Each new document you create during a session in Word is given a temporary name following the Document1 format. Your second document will be called Document2, the next one Document3 and so on. These names should be considered temporary – you will save your document and give it a meaningful name instead of the temporary name assigned by Word.

The insertion point – the flashing black vertical bar – is in the top left of the text area on the first page. You're ready to start – just type!

Things to remember when entering text into your document:

- DO NOT press [Enter] at the end of each line of text. If a sentence is going to run onto a new line, let it – the text will be wrapped automatically at the end of the line.
- DO press [Enter] at the end of short lines of text, e.g. after lines in an address at the top of a letter or after the last line in a paragraph.
- To leave a clear line between paragraphs, or several empty lines between headings or in the signature block at the end of a letter, press [Enter] as often as is necessary to get the effect you want.

3.2 Moving the insertion point

When you need to fix a mistake, the first thing you have to do is place the insertion point next to the error.

If necessary, use the scroll bars to bring the text you want to edit into view.

There are several different ways of moving the insertion point. Experiment with the various options as you work.

Using the mouse:

❶ Position the I-beam (the name given to mouse pointer shape when it is over a text area) at the place you want to move the insertion point to.

❷ Click the left mouse button.

Using the keyboard:

To move a character or line at a time	→, ←, ↑, ↓
To move right or left a word at a time	[Ctrl] → or ←
To move up or down a paragraph at a time	[Ctrl] ↑ or ↓
To move to the end of the line	[End]
To move to the beginning of the line	[Home]
To move to the beginning of the document	[Ctrl]-[Home]
To move to the end of the document	[Ctrl]-[End]

3.3   Editing

To insert new text:

❶   Position the insertion point where you want the new text to appear.

❷   Type in your new text.

To delete existing text:

❶   Position the insertion point next to the character that you want to delete.

❷   To delete characters to the *left*, press the [←] backspace key once for each character.

Or

❸   To delete characters to the *right,* press the [Delete] key once for each character.

Both the [←] backspace and [Delete] keys repeat – if you hold them down they will zoom through your text removing it much quicker than you could type it in, so be careful with them!

Overtype

You can type over existing text, replacing the old text with the new in one operation, instead of deleting the old then entering the new. Press the [Insert] key to switch overtype on and off.

◆   When Overtype mode is on, the text on the Overtype button `OVR` on the Status bar is black.

❶   Switch on Overtype mode – press [Insert].

❷   Position the insertion point within some existing text and type – watch to see what happens. The existing text will be replaced with the new text you enter.

❸   Switch Overtype mode off again – press [Insert].

To insert a new paragraph:

❶   Position the insertion point where the paragraph break should be and press [Enter] – twice if you want to leave a blank line.

To join two paragraphs:

❶   Delete the [Enter] characters between the paragraphs.

Experiment! You could type:

- a letter to a friend
- some notes on a hobby you pursue
- a future best-selling novel!

3.4 Page breaks

As you type in your text a page break is inserted automatically when you reach the end of your page.

However, if you want a page break to occur at a specific point, e.g. at the end of a chapter or topic, you can insert a forced page break.

To insert a forced page break:

❶ Position the insertion point where the break should be inserted.

❷ Press [Ctrl]-[Enter].

3.5 Special characters and symbols

Most of the characters you want to type into your document are available through the keyboard. However, there may be times when you want a character that is not on the keyboard. You may find the character required in the **Symbols** dialog box.

To insert a symbol:

❶ Position the insertion point where you want the character to appear.

❷ Open the **Insert** menu.

❸ Choose **Symbol**.

❹ Select the font you wish to select a character from (you'll need to spend some time exploring the fonts you have available).

❺ Select a character – click on it.

❻ Click **Insert**.

❼ Click **Close** to close the dialog box.

3.6 View options

When working in a document, there are several view options available. The view option you select controls how your document looks on the screen – not how it will print out. You will usually work in Normal view or Print Layout view when entering text.

Normal view

Normal view is the default view for working in Word. It is the view usually used for entering, editing and formatting text. The page layout is simplified in Normal view – margins, headers and footers, multiple columns, pictures, etc. – are not displayed.

To change to Normal view:

❶   Open the **View** menu and choose **Normal**.

Or

❷   Click the **Normal View** tool ▤ at the bottom left of the screen.

Print Layout view

In this view you can see where your objects will be positioned on the page. Your margins are displayed (and any headers or footers you have within them), and pictures, drawings, multiple columns, etc. are all displayed in their true position on the page.

Print Layout view is useful if you are working with headers and footers, altering margins, working in columns, or are combining text and graphics on a page and wish to see how they will be placed relative to each other.

To change to Print Layout view:

❶   Open the **View** menu and choose **Print Layout**.

Or

❷   Click the **Print Layout View** tool ▣ at the bottom left of the screen.

The other view options are Web Layout view and Outline view. You don't need to know how to use these views at this stage, but have a look at them if you wish. If you go into Web Layout view the View tools at the bottom left of the screen disappear.

♦   You can use the **View** menu to get back to Normal or Print Layout view from Web Layout view.

Zoom

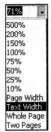

You can also change the zoom (magnification) options when viewing your document. Click the drop down arrow at the Zoom tool on the Standard toolbar and select an option from the list.

♦   Open one of your documents and experiment with the view options.

3.7   Selection techniques

Selection techniques are *very* important in Word. You need to use them if you want to:

♦   copy or move text within a document

♦   copy or move text from one document to another

♦   change the formatting of existing text

♦   quickly delete large chunks of text.

There are several ways to select text in Word – try some out and use whatever seems easiest for you.

Using the mouse	
Any amount of text	Click and drag over it
Any amount of text	Click at the beginning of text, hold the [Shift] key down, click at the end of text
A word	Double click on it
A sentence	Hold down the [Ctrl] key and click anywhere within the sentence
A paragraph	Double click in the selection bar to the left of the paragraph you wish to select *or* triple click anywhere within the paragraph
The whole document	Triple click in the selection bar

To deselect any unit of text:

♦   Click anywhere within your text, or press one of the arrow keys on your keyboard.

Using the keyboard	
To select a character or line at a time	Hold the [Shift] key down and press the right, left, up or down arrow keys
To select right or left, a word at a time	Hold down the [Shift] and [Ctrl] keys and press the right or left arrow key
To select up or down a paragraph at a time	Hold down the [Shift] and [Ctrl] keys and press the up or down arrow key
To select to the end of the line	[Shift]-[End]
To select to the beginning of the line	[Shift]-[Home]
To select to the beginning of the document	[Shift]-[Ctrl]-[Home]
To select to the end of the document	[Shift]-[Ctrl]-[End]
To select the whole document	[Ctrl]-[A]

Don't be afraid to experiment with the different selection techniques. Many of the keyboard ones are much more efficient than the usual click and drag method.

3.8 Font formatting

Standard formatting routines are used when formatting characters in Word (see 8.7).

Explore the **Font** dialog box to see what other font formatting options are available.

❶ Open the **Format** menu and choose **Font**.

❷ Select the **Font** tab.

❸ Choose the effects you want – a preview of your selection is displayed in the Preview window.

❹   Click **OK** to apply the effects to your text, or **Cancel** to return to
    your document without making any changes.

3.9   Paragraph formatting

Some formatting options are applied to complete paragraphs, regardless of
whether the paragraph consists of a few words or several lines. A paragraph is created in Word each time you press the [Enter] key.

Line spacing

Initially, your line spacing is set to single. You can easily change to double
or 1½ line spacing if you wish.

You can set the line spacing with the keyboard shortcuts:

*   Double line spacing   [Ctrl] – [2]
*   1½ line spacing   [Ctrl] – [5]
*   Single line spacing   [Ctrl] – [1]

Bulleted and Numbered Lists

You can easily add bullets or numbers automatically to your paragraphs.

❶   Click the **Bullets** tool 📋 to switch bullets on or off.

❷   Click the **Numbering** tool 📋 to switch the numbers on or off.

To change the bullet or number style:

❶   Select the paragraphs you want bulleted.
❷   Open the **Format** menu and choose **Bullets and Numbering**.
❸   Select the **Bulleted** or **Numbered** tab in the dialog box.
❹   Choose a bullet or numbering option from those displayed.
❺   Click **OK**.

Indents

Your paragraphs normally run the full width of your typing line – from the left margin to the right margin. As you enter your text, it extends along the line until it reaches the right margin and then it automatically wraps to the next line (unless you press the [Enter] key.)

To increase the indent of all lines in a paragraph from the left margin:

♦ Click the **Increase Indent** tool ▣ on the Formatting toolbar.

To decrease the indent of all lines in a paragraph from the left margin:

♦ Click the **Decrease Indent** tool ▣ on the Formatting toolbar,

Changing the indents using the horizontal ruler

You can also use the ruler to set your indents. The ruler must be displayed along the top of your text area – if it's not, open the View menu and choose Ruler to display it.

The indent markers are the two triangles and the small rectangle below them at the left edge of the ruler, and the small triangle at the right.

To adjust the indent of:

♦ The first line in the paragraph from the left margin, drag the top triangle at the left edge of the ruler.

♦ All other lines (except the first line) in the paragraph from the left margin, drag the bottom triangle at the left edge.

♦ All lines in the paragraph from the left margin, drag the rectangle below the two triangles at the left.

♦ All lines in the paragraph from the right margin, drag the triangle at the right edge of the ruler.

To set the indent you require:

♦ Drag the appropriate indent marker along the ruler into position.

To help improve accuracy when setting indents using the ruler, you can display the exact position of your indent on the ruler as you drag it along.

♦ Hold the [Alt] key down while you click and drag.

Tabs

Tabs are used to align your text horizontally on the typing line. If you want to type up a list of names and telephone numbers you can use tabs to align each column.

The default tabs are set every half inch along the ruler – the small dark grey marks along the bottom edge of the ruler indicate their positions.

Each time you press the [Tab] key the insertion point jumps forward to the next tab position that is set. The default tabs have left alignment – when you enter your text or numbers the left edge of the text or data entered is at the tab position.

Tabs can be aligned to the left, right, centre or decimal point character.

Alignment	Effect	Possible use
Left	The left edge is at tab	Any text or numbers
Right	The right edge is at tab	Text, or numbers you want to line up on the unit
Centre	Centred under the tab	Anything
Decimal	Decimal point under tab	Figures that you want to line up on the decimal point

If you need to use tabs and the pre-set ones are not what you require, you must set tabs at the positions you need them.

To set a tab using the ruler:

❶   Select the type of tab required – click the style button to the left of the ruler until you've got the alignment option required

   ⊾ Left   ⊥ Centre   ⅃ Right   ⅃ Decimal

❷   Point to the lower half of the ruler and click – your tab is set

To move a tab:

♦   Drag it along the ruler to its correct position.

To delete a tab:

♦   Drag it *down* off the ruler, and drop it.

To set tabs in the **Tabs** dialog box:

❶ Open the **Format** menu and choose **Tabs**.

❷ Enter the Tab stop position.

❸ Select the alignment.

❹ Choose a **Leader** character if wanted.

❹ Click **Set**.

❺ Repeat to set all your tabs.

❻ Click **OK**.

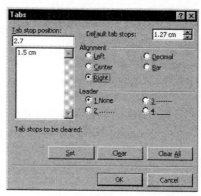

Leader character ... set to tab

EX𝒫ERIM𝔼NT

3.10 Print preview and print

See 8.11 for standard preview and print information. When you preview your file a full page is displayed at a time. You can zoom in and out so that you can read the text, and you can edit your text if you wish.

Zoom

If you move your mouse pointer over your page in print preview, you will notice it looks like a magnifying glass with a + on it.

◆ Position the mouse pointer over your page and click the left mouse button and you will be *zoomed* in and out of your document.

Editing text in print preview

If you zoom in on your text, and notice something that you want to change, you can edit your document in print preview.

- Click the **Magnifier** tool  on the Print Preview toolbar.

The insertion point will appear in your document. Edit your document and click the Magnifier tool again so that you can zoom in and out.

Print

If you are happy with the appearance of your document, and want to print it from the preview window, click the **Print** tool  on the Print Preview toolbar. One copy of the document will be printed.

Print Preview toolbar

The Print Preview window has its own toolbar which can be used to control the display of your document on the screen.

Experiment with the tools to see what effect they have.

From left to right on the toolbar, ignoring the print and magnifier tools discussed above, you have:

One Page – click to display one page of the document on screen at a time.

Multiple Pages – drops down a grid that you can click and drag over to indicate the number of pages you want to display at one time – maximum number 6 across and 2 down.

Zoom – sets the percentage of magnification on your document.

View Ruler – toggles the display of the vertical and horizontal rulers.

Shrink to Fit – if a small amount of text appears on the last page of your document you may be able to reduce the number of pages by clicking this tool. Word decreases the size of each font used in the document to get the text to fit on to one page less.

Full Screen – removes most of the toolbars, menu bar, title bar, etc. to get a 'clean screen' display. To return the screen to normal, click **Close Full Screen** on the Full Screen toolbar or press [Esc].

Close Preview – exits Print Preview and returns you to your document.

Context Sensitive Help – click this, then click on a tool, scroll bar, ruler, etc. to get a brief description of its function. Once you've read the information, click anywhere on your screen to close the information box.

Moving through your document in Print Preview

If you have more than one page in your document, you may want to scroll through the pages in Print Preview to check them. To do this:

♦ Click the arrows at the top or bottom of the vertical scroll bar.

Or

♦ Click the **Previous Page** or **Next Page** button at the bottom of the vertical scroll bar.

Print

If you don't want to print the whole document, you can specify the pages to print in the **Print** dialog box. You can also set the number of copies here.

❶ Open the **File** menu and choose **Print**.

❷ Select the **Page range** – *All*, *Current page* (the one the insertion point is in) or *Pages*, e.g.1,2,4-7,12.

♦ If you have selected some text before displaying the dialog box, the *Selection* option becomes active so that you can print out just the text that is selected.

❸ Set the number of copies required – usually one.

❹ Click **OK**.

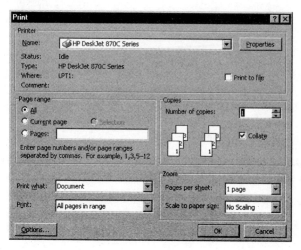

3.11   Find and Replace

If you're working on a longer document and want to find some text that you know you've typed in, you could use the Find command to help you find it (rather than scroll through the pages looking for it).

To find a piece of text:

❶   Open the **Edit** menu and choose **Find...**

❷   Enter the text you want to find in the **Find what:** field.

❸   Complete the other search options as required – the options can be toggled by clicking the **Less/More** button.

❹   Click **Find Next**. Word will highlight the first occurrence of the text it finds.

❺   If necessary, click **Find Next** to move on to the next occurrence.

❻   When the appropriate text has been located click **Cancel** to return to your document.

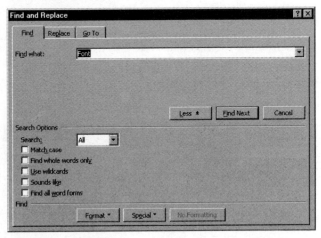

To replace a piece of text:

If you've typed something incorrectly several times, e.g. 'Mr Donaldson' when it should have been 'Mrs Peterson' use the Replace feature to fix it.

❶   Open the **Edit** menu and choose **Replace...**

❷   Complete the Replace tab with details of the text you want to find and replace in the **Find what:** and **Replace with:** fields.

❸ Select any other options required.

❹ Click **Find Next**.

◆ Word will highlight the first occurrence of the text it finds.

❺ Click **Replace** to replace this one occurrence, then click **Find Next** again.

Or

◆ Click **Replace All** to get all occurrences replaced automatically.

3.12 Word templates

A *template* is a pattern on which a document is based. You have probably been creating documents using the *Blank Document* template – you simply click the **New** tool on the Standard toolbar to create a document based on it. The document created has an A4 paper size, portrait orientation, 1" top and bottom margin, 1.25" left and right margin and single line spacing. Paragraph and character styles that are part of the Blank Document template are available in the style list on the Formatting toolbar (see 3.13).

Word comes with several other templates ready for you to use. You should look through these templates as you may find some of them useful. There are templates for letters, memos, fax, résumés (CV) and many other types of document.

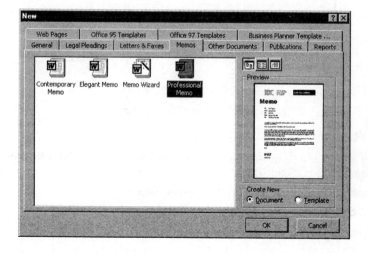

To create a document using a different Word template:

❶   Open the **File** menu and choose **New**.

❷   Select a tab to display the templates available in each category (the *Blank Document* template is on the **General** tab).

❸   Choose a template.

❹   Click **OK**.

Explore the document that you have created. Check out the layout – notice that some templates, e.g. memo and fax, include areas for your company name, address, telephone/fax number, etc.

Many of the documents created using a Word template include details on how to use and complete the document that you have created.

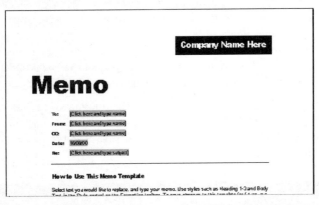

In the main, you just follow the instructions on the screen. Select and replace pieces of text that prompt you for your own details, e.g. **Company Name Here**.

With other prompts, e.g. **[Click here and type name]**, etc. just do as you're told – click in the highlighted area and enter your information.

Your own Word templates

If you find a template that you would like to use, you can customize it with your company or personal details and save the customized template for future use.

If you have a standard layout, e.g. your own memo or letterhead layout, you should save the basic layout as a template.

To create your own template:

❶ Create a new document using the template you wish to customize and enter your own company name, address, etc.

Or

♦ Create a new blank document and set up the layout, standard text, etc. for your template. Page Setup (3.14), headers and footers (3.15), styles (3.13), etc. can all be set up to suit your requirements.

❷ Open the **File** menu and choose **Save As...**

❸ In the **Save as type** field, choose *Document Template*.

❹ Select the folder in which you wish to store your template – choose either the *Templates* folder or one of its sub-folders.

❺ Give your template a name.

❻ Click **Save**.

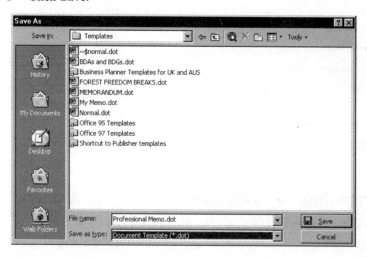

Experiment!

Try out some of the templates on your system – they may help you produce a very professional looking document easily.

3.13 Styles

As an alternative to formatting your text manually (using the Formatting toolbar or the dialog boxes) you could format text using a set of formatting options that have already been set up in a *style*. Each new Word document will have several styles already set up. The text you have entered into your documents has been formatted using the *Normal* style – Times New Roman, size 12, left aligned.

To display the styles available in your current document:

♦   Click the drop down arrow to the right of the **Style** box on the Formatting toolbar.

Many styles are already set up in Word – far more than those displayed in the style list. Different styles are recorded in the various templates and are automatically available to you when you create a document using these templates.

To apply a style to new text:

❶   Click the drop down arrow to the right of the **Style** box to display the style list.

❷   Select the style you want to use – click on it.

❸   Type in your text.

❹   Press [Enter].

Heading 1 – Arial, size 14, bold, left aligned, spacing before 12 pt, spacing after 3 pt

Normal – Times New Roman, size 12, spacing before and after 0 pt

Heading 2 – Arial, size 12, bold, italic, left aligned, spacing before 12 pt, spacing after 3 pt

Heading 3 – Arial, size 12, left aligned, spacing before 12 pt, spacing after 3 pt

When you press [Enter] after each of the Heading styles, the paragraph style used for the *following paragraph* returns to Normal automatically.

To apply a style to existing text:

❶ Select the text you want to apply a style to.

❷ Click the drop down arrow to the right of the **Style** box to display the style list.

❸ Select the style you want to use.

Styles are magic! They'll help you achieve a consistent look within and across your documents. You can also set up your own styles – check out the online help.

3.14 Page Setup

You can change the page setup for all or part of your document. Initially, documents based on the default template consist of one *section*. If you select **Apply to:** *This Point Forward* when changing the page layout as discussed below, Word creates a new section. Each section in a document can have different margins, orientation, page size, etc. If your document has more than one section the **Apply to:** field in the **Page Setup** dialog box contains three options – *Whole document, This point forward* and *This section* – so that you can modify the layout of existing sections. The section number of the section that the insertion point is currently in is displayed at the left of the Status Bar, beside the page number.

Margins

To change the margin setting:

❶ Open the **File** menu and choose **Page Setup...**

❷ Select the **Margins** tab.

❸ Edit the margin fields as required.

❹ Specify the area of your document you want to apply the changes to in the **Apply to:** field *Whole document, This point forward* or *This section*.

❺ Click **OK**.

Orientation

The orientation of a page can be Portrait or Landscape. The default orientation is Portrait. You can change the orientation of your pages for all of your document or for part of it as required.

To change orientation:

❶   Open the **File** menu and choose **Page Setup...**

❷   Select the **Paper Size** tab.

❸   Choose the orientation.

❹   Specify the area of your document you want to apply the changes to in the **Apply to:** field.

❺   Click **OK**.

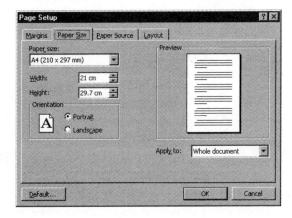

Page size

If you are not printing onto A4 size paper, you may need to change the page size setting so that Word will insert page breaks in the correct place.

To change the page size:

❶   Open the **File** menu and choose **Page Setup...**

❷   Select the **Paper Size** tab.

❸   Choose the **Paper Size**.

❹   Specify the area of your document you want to apply the changes to in the **Apply to:** field.

❺   Click **OK**.

3.15 Headers/footers

Headers and footers are displayed at the top and bottom of each page in your document. They usually contain things like page numbers, the name of the author, the filename or the date that the document was produced.

To insert a header or footer:

❶   Open the **View** menu.

❷   Choose **Header and Footer**.

✦   The insertion point moves to the header area.

✦   The main document text is dimmed.

✦   The header and footer area has a centre tab set in the middle of the line and a right tab at the end. You can use these to help you position your text and/or page numbers.

You can type any text you wish into the header and footer areas. Use the tabs to help you position the insertion point as necessary.

You can format your text in the same way as you format text in the main document area.

The Header and Footer toolbar is displayed – use the tools on it to insert fields that will be completed and updated automatically by Word.

Header and footer tools

Insert AutoText   – insert filename, author name, etc.

[#]   **Page Number**   – inserts automatic page numbering.

[¹]   **Total Number of Pages** – inserts the total number of pages in the document.

[⧉]   **Format Page Number** – alternative formats for page numbers.

[⧉]   **Insert Date**   – inserts the date that the document is printed.

[⊘]   **Insert Time** – inserts the time that the document is printed.

[⧉]   **Page Setup** – opens the **Header and footer** dialog box.

Show/hide document text – toggles the display of the document text.

Same as Previous – makes/breaks link between headers and footers in different sections of a document.

Switch between header and footer – switches between the header and footer area.

Show Next – displays the next header or footer in document (if document divided into sections).

Show Previous – displays the previous header or footer in document (if document divided into sections).

Close – returns you to your document.

♦ You can also number your pages by choosing **Page Numbers...** from the **Insert** menu and selecting the options required from the dialog box.

Always use headers and footers for text or numbers that you want at the top or bottom of every page. *Never* type them into the main text area!

3.16 Tables

Tables are used to help you arrange text and data in columns on your page. Tables consist of rows and columns. Where a row and column intersect, we have a cell.

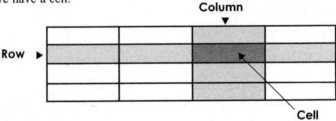

To create a table:

❶ Place the insertion point where you want your table to appear.

❷ Click the **Insert Table** tool on the **Standard** toolbar.

❸ Click and drag over the grid that appears until you get the number of rows and columns required.

❹ Let go the mouse button – you have an empty table on your page.

You can move around your table using the keyboard or the mouse.

* Press the [Tab] key to move forward to the next cell.

* Hold [Shift] down and press [Tab] to move to the previous cell.

Or

* Click in the cell you want to move to.

Selecting cells in a table:

* Click and drag over the cells you want to select.

Or

❶ Click in the corner cell of the range of cells you want to select.

❷ Point to the cell in the diagonally opposite corner using your mouse.

❸ Hold [Shift] down and click.

To select a column:

* Click the **top** gridline or border of the column you want to select (you should get a black arrow pointing downwards).

* To select several adjacent columns, click and drag along the top border.

To select a row:

* Click to the **left** of the row you want to select.

* To select several adjacent rows, click and drag up or down the row selector area (to the left of the table).

To select a cell:

* Click just inside the **left** edge of the cell.

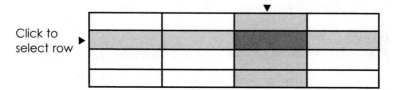

Click to select column

Click to select row

Other things to note:

- ◆ When entering text into a cell, you will find that it automatically wraps once the text reaches the right edge of the cell, and the row deepens to accommodate the text you are entering (provided you have spaces between the words, or you pressed [Enter]).

- ◆ If you press [Tab] when the insertion point is in the last cell in the last row of your table, a new row is created.

- ◆ You can format your cells, or text within the cells, using the normal formatting commands, e.g. bold, italic, colour, size, alignment (note that your text is aligned *within* the cell), borders and shading, etc.

Column width

In most cases, you won't want all your columns to be the same width – it depends upon what you're entering. You can change the width as required. There are several methods you might like to try, then use whatever you find easiest. The insertion point must be within a table when using these.

AutoFit:

You must have some text or data in your columns to give AutoFit something to work on.

- ◆ Double click the border or gridline to the right of the column whose width you want to change.

You will also find a number of **AutoFit** options in the **Table** menu. Experiment with them to see how the different options work.

Manual adjustment:

- ❶ Position the pointer over the gridline to the right of the column you want to adjust, below the top horizontal gridline of the table.

- ❷ Click and drag the border or gridline as required.

Or

- ❶ Click and drag the **Move Table Column** marker (on the ruler) which is above the right border of the column you want to adjust.

Hotel	Address	Prices
Old Mill Inn	24 Mill Lane Melrose	Dinner £35: Single Room £30 Double Room £45
Kathy's Kitchen	12 High Street Duns	Lunch from £6. High Tea from £10/head

Insert and delete rows and columns

You may find that you need to insert (or delete) rows or columns.

To insert a row:

❶ Select the row that will be above the new row.

❷ Right click on the selected area.

❸ Choose **Insert Rows** from the shortcut menu.

To insert a column within a table:

❶ Select the column that will be to the right of the new column.

❷ Right click on the selected area.

❸ Choose **Insert Columns** from the shortcut menu.

You may find that you have to adjust the width of your columns to accommodate the new columns you add.

To delete a row or column:

❶ Select the row or column that you want to delete.

❷ Right click on the selected area.

❸ Select **Delete Rows** or **Delete Columns** (the option displayed depends on what you selected at step 1).

To delete an entire table:

❶ Place the insertion point anywhere inside the table.

❷ Open the **Table** menu and choose **Delete**.

❸ Click **Table**.

♦ If you select some cells in your table then press the [Delete] key , the *contents* of the table are deleted, but the table remains in place.

♦ Experiment with the options in the Table menu and display the Tables & Borders toolbar and experiment with the tools on it.

Table Autoformat

You can format the text, data and cells within your table using the formatting toolbar and the dialog boxes. However, there are a number of table *Autoformats* that you can use to quickly format your table.

❶ Click anywhere inside your table.

❷ Choose **Table Autoformat** from the **Table** menu.

❸ Select an **Autoformat** from the dialog box.

❹ Select or deselect the checkboxes until you have the formatting options required.

❺ Click **OK**.

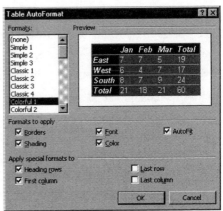

Tables are brilliant! They make presenting text and data in columns easy, and can be used to produce excellent forms!

3.17 Mail merge

You can combine the text and/or layout of a standard document (e.g. letter or labels) with a set of variables (usually names and addresses) to produce a personalized document using mail merge. The letters that you receive from banks, building societies and sales organizations, etc. which are promoting services and products, and are personalized with your name and address, are often the result of a mail merge.

Mail merge jargon

Main document – the document that contains the layout, standard text and field names that point to the data source.

Data source – the file that contains the records you require for your mail merge – perhaps a name and address file. The data source is usually in a table layout – it could be a Word file or a table in Access or Excel if you have them installed. Other data sources can be used – see the on-line Help for details. We will create our data source in Word.

Record – the set of information on each item in your data source.

Field – a piece of data within a record. Title, surname, first name, telephone number, etc. would be held in separate fields.

Field name – the name used to identify a field.

Result document – the document produced when you combine the records in the data source with the main document.

There are three steps involved in mail merge:

❶ Creating the **main document**.

❷ Creating and/or locating the **data source**.

❸ Merging the two to produce the **result document**.

Experiment by setting up a merge letter and labels following the guidelines below. You could do a standard letter inviting people to a meeting, or a party. Or set up a 'thank you' letter – might be handy at Christmas!

Creating a letter for the main document

You can create a main document from scratch or use an existing document.

❶ Create a new document (or open an existing document) – this will become your letter.

❷ Open the **Tools** menu and choose **Mail Merge...**

❸ Choose **Create**, then **Form Letters** at step 1 in the **Mail Merge Helper dialog** box.

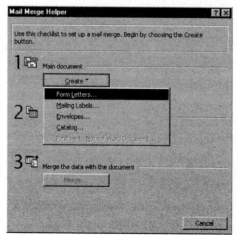

❹   Select **Active Window** at the prompt. An **Edit** button now appears
     at step 1.

❺   Click the **Edit** button then select the file name you wish to edit.

❻   Type up/edit your main document as required.

❼   **Save** your main document.

To create your data source file

❶   Open the **Tools** menu and choose **Mail Merge...**

❷   Click the **Get Data...** button at step 2.

❸   Choose **Create Data Source...**   so you can set up your data file (if
     the Data Source already exists, choose Get Data... and open the
     data source file).

◆   The **Create Data Source** dialog box appears.

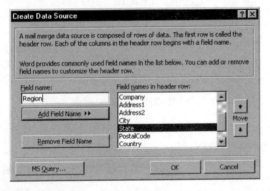

Word automatically presents a list of the field names it suggests for the
header row in your data source file. These are the *field names* for your
data.

❶   Modify the header row list as required.

To add a field name:

◆   Enter the field name (single words only – no spaces) in the **Field
     name** slot and click the **Add Field Name** button.

To remove a field name:

◆   Select the field name you don't require from the **Field names in
     header row** list, and click the **Remove Field Name** button.

To rearrange the order of the field names:

❶   Select the field name you want to move in the **Field names in header row** list, and click the arrow buttons to the right of the list to move the field name up or down.

❷   Click **OK** once you've got the header row arranged as required.

❸   Give the file a suitable name at the **Save As** dialog box, leave the file type at *Word Document* and click **Save**.

❹   Choose **Edit Data Source** to add your records.

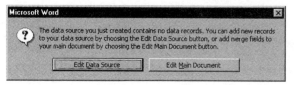

To enter data:

❶   Enter the data for the first record into the **Data Form**.

◆   Press [Tab] to move from field to field.

❷   Click **Add New** when you've completed one record and you want a new empty Data Form to complete.

◆   Use the navigation buttons at the bottom of the Data Form to move through your records to check them.

❸   Click **View Source** when you've finished – this displays your data source file in a table layout.

❹   **Save** your file.

DATA FORM AND DATA SOURCE

It is usually easier to add and edit records in your data source file using the Data Form as the front end to your file – the table layout isn't as user friendly. However, you must return to the source document to save your file – click the View Source button in the Data Form.

To display the Data Form again click the Data Form tool on the Database toolbar.

Complete the main document

Once your data source file is ready, you can complete the main document.

Move to the main document from the data source file:

❶   If the Data Form is displayed, click the **View Source** button.

❷   Click the **Mail Merge Main Document** tool on the Database toolbar.

Your main document will contain:

♦   Standard text for your letter.

♦   Formatting and layout options as required.

We must now add the field names from the data source – so that Word can insert the detail from each record in the correct place in the letter.

To complete your main document:

❶   Modify the page setup, tabs, etc. and enter or edit standard text if necessary.

❷   Position the insertion point where you wish to insert data from the data source file.

❸   Click the **Insert Merge Field** button on the Mail Merge toolbar to display the list of field names.

❹   Select the field name that contains the data from the **Insert Merge Field** list (the contents of the field in the data source file will appear when you produce the result document).

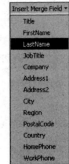

 ◆   A merge field can be included several times in the same main docu-
     ment if wanted – as in the address and salutation of this example.

 ◆   Use the spacebar and/or [Enter] key to lay out fields as required.

 ❺   Repeat 3–4 above until all the fields required are in place in the
     main document.

 ❻   **Save** the main document.

The   field   names
appear within << >> in
your main document.

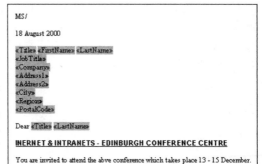

If the field codes
appear {MERGEFIELD
Fieldname}   it   is
because the option to
view the field codes is
switched on. Press
[Alt]-[F9] to toggle the
display of the codes.

The result document

Once your main document and data source file have been set up, you can
produce your result document. There are several options to choose from
when merging the data from the data source file with the main document
– try them out to see how they work.

To get a better idea of how the result document will look, you can merge
the data of an individual record and view it on screen.

 ❶   Click the **View Merged Data** tool ⬛ – the data from the first
     data record will be displayed in the main document.

 ❷   Use the **First Record**, **Previous Record**, **Next Record**, **Last
     Record** tools on the Mail Merge toolbar to display data from other
     records if you want to – or enter the record number you want to
     display in the **Go To Record** box and press [Enter].

 ◆   To print the main document with the data currently displayed, click
     the **Print** tool on the Standard toolbar.

 ◆   Click the **View Merged Data** tool to display the field codes again.

Merging all the records

You can collect the result documents into a new document before you print, or you can send the results of the merge directly to your printer.

To collect the result documents into a new document:

❶ Display the main document.

❷ Click the **Merge to New Document** tool .

If you want to add information to some of the result documents before you print, use this method and edit your new document as required.

◆ To print the new result document, click the **Print** tool on the Standard toolbar.

To output a result document directly to the printer:

❶ Display the main document.

❷ Click the **Merge to Printer** tool.

◆ Close your files when you've finished working with them.

◆ Create a new main document or open an existing one and perform a mail merge using the name and address file you have set up.

Mailing labels

You can create labels by merging a label layout with your name and address file:

❶ Start a new blank document and open the **Tools** menu and choose **Mail Merge...**

❷ Choose **Create**, then **Mailing Labels** at step 1 and select **Active Window** at the prompt.

❸ Click **Get Data...** (assuming that the data file already exists).

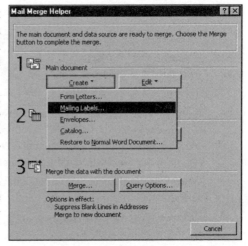

❹ Choose **Open Data Source...** and open the name and address file you wish to use.

❺ At step 1 of the **Mail Merge Helper** dialog box, click **Setup...**

❻ Select a label layout and click **OK**.

❼ Insert the fields required into your label – remember to press [Spacebar] or [Enter] to get the layout required – then click **OK**.

❽ At the **Mail Merge Helper** dialog box, click **Merge...**

❾ Choose **New Document** or **Printer** at the Merge to field (remember to load your label stationery).

❿ Click **Merge**.

Use mail merge to:
* prepare invitations to a party
* write thank you letters
* apply for jobs.

3.18   Importing objects

Insert File

To import a spreadsheet or chart into Word:

❶ Open the **Insert** menu and choose **File...**

❷ Locate and select the workbook that contains the data or chart that you want to import and click **Insert**.

❸ Choose **Entire Workbook**, or click the drop down arrow and select the sheet required.

❹ Complete the **Name or Cell Range** field as required.

❺ Click **OK**.

* Data is inserted as a Word table and can be edited in Word using table handling features.

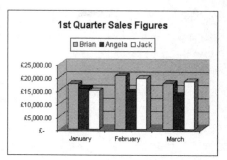

You can also copy text, data, graphics, charts, etc. from one application to another within the Office suite using simple copy and paste techniques.

Copy and paste

❶   Launch Word and the application you want to copy from.

❷   Select the object, text or data you want to copy.

❸   Click the **Copy** tool on the Standard toolbar.

❹   Switch to Word.

❺   Place the insertion point where you want the object, text or data to appear.

❻   Click the **Paste** tool.

Sales Figures - 1st quarter				
	January	February	March	Total
Brian	£17,500.00	£20,500.00	£17,600.00	£ 55,600.00
Angela	£15,600.00	£14,320.00	£13,059.00	£ 42,979.00
Jack	£14,780.00	£19,500.00	£18,300.00	£ 52,580.00

> Remember to check Chapter 8 for other areas that may be tested, e.g. importing pictures, drawing objects, etc.

3.19   Mock test

Read *The tests* section in the Preface before you start. Each of the 30 tasks in the test is allocated 1 mark. In the ECDL test the files will be provided on disk, but in order to practise, you could type and save the 2 files below.

Preparation

Use the font Courier New (or similar), size 10. Type the files in *exactly* as they are shown below. Type in and save the first file as *Orkney.doc* then close it.

```
William Watson
15 Hill View Crescent
Stromness
Orkney
```

To the members of the Festival committee. Wednesday 4 October 2000.

The first meeting for the Festival committee preparing the 2001 event (7-14 July 2001) will be Wednesday 25 October 2000 at 7.30 in the village hall.

                              Agenda

Current funds
Fund raising initiatives
Election of office bearers - the chairman and treas-
urer
Draft programme of events for week
Allocation of duties
School liaison
Local enterprise liaison
Election of the auditor
Any other competent business

Enter the following data into a separate file. The file should be a data
document that can be used in a mail merge. Save this file as *nameadd.doc*
and close it.

Name	Address	Town
Peter Jackson	22 High Street	Stromness
Alison Dickson	10 Queen's Crescent	Stromness
John Robson	2a River View	Stromness
Paula Andrews	14 Main Street	Kirkwall

Exit Word before you attempt the mock test. Remember to time yourself –
45 minutes tops!

Test

In this test you will be given a draft circular letter for the local festival
committee. You must edit the letter as instructed then use it in a mail
merge with the names and addresses in your address list.

1. Open the word processing application.

2. Open the document *Orkney.doc.* The document is an unedited version of the circular.

3. Save the document onto your test disk using the filename *festival circular.doc*

4. Select all the text in the document and change the font in the document to Times New Roman.

5. Left align the word *Agenda.*

6. Make the word *Agenda* bold.

7. Change the font size of the word *Agenda* to 20 points.

8. Move the date of the circular *Wednesday 4 October 2000* above *William Watson*, and leave two clear lines between the date and the name.

9. Right align the date of the circular *Wednesday 4 October 2000.*

10. Move the item *Election of office bearers – the chairman and treasurer* to the top of the list.

11. Delete *and treasurer* from the item that you have just moved.

12. Number the Agenda items – keep the numbering flush with the left margin.

13. Set the line spacing between the agenda items to 1.5.

14. Type the words *Festival Committee* centred, in the header of the document.

15. At the bottom of the page, below the Agenda items, insert two blank lines and then insert the text *On behalf of the Committee William Watson* on the third line below the last agenda item.

16. Use the left tab to align the words *On behalf of the Committee* at 2.5 cm from the left margin and *William Watson* at 8.5 cm.

17. Insert a page break after *William Watson* at the bottom of page.

18. Type the following text at the top of the new page: *Notes from Meeting.*

19. Indent the text, *Notes from Meeting,* to start at 3 cm to the right of the left margin.

20. Insert page numbers at the foot of your document (do not use Footers to carry out this task), ensure that the numbers are centre aligned.

21. Insert a Clip Art picture from a Clip Gallery on the first page of the document below the last line of text: *On behalf of the Committee William Watson.*

22. Resize the picture so that it will fill the bottom of the first page.

23. Use a spell-check program and make changes if necessary. (Proper names are not included in this spell checking and may be ignored.)

24. Save the document and print two copies of the first page to an output printer if available, or as a print file to your disk.

25. Mail Merge: Use the file *festival circular.doc* and create a form letter.

26. Open the file *nameadd.doc.* It contains an address list that is going to be used as a data source and merged with the *festival circular.doc* form letter.

27. Enter three merge fields into the *festival circular.doc* document: Substitute the three text lines

    William Watson   (upper left corner of the circular)

    15 Hill View Crescent

    Stromness.

    with the following fields in the document.

    <<Name>>

    <<Address>>

    <<Town>>

28. Merge the address list with *festival circular.doc* to create the resulting document.

29. Save the merged document in Rich Text Format (*rtf*) as *orkmrge.rtf* to your disk.

30. Save all the documents and close the application.

SUMMARY

The chapter has discussed the features in Word that you should be able to use. We have discussed:

✓ View options.

✓ Paragraph formatting options including bullets, numbering, tabs, indents, etc.

✓ Headers and footers.

✓ Page numbering – using headers and footers, and using Insert, Page Numbers...

✓ Templates.

✓ Styles.

✓ Tables.

✓ Mail Merge.

✓ Importing data from other applications.

4 | SPREADSHEETS

AIMS OF THIS CHAPTER

This chapter discusses the areas that you must become familiar with in Excel before you are ready to attempt the ECDL Module 4 test, Spreadsheets. Entering text and data, formatting, formulas and functions are covered in detail. Sorting, absolute addressing, and charts are also discussed. Refer to Chapter 8 for information on features that are standard (or pretty standard) across the applications.

4.1 The Excel screen

Whichever method you choose to start Excel, you are presented with a new workbook displaying a blank worksheet. Areas of the screen that are specific to Excel are labelled in the screenshot opposite.

* If the workbook window is maximized, the workbook and the application share one Title bar containing the application and workbook names.

4.2 Workbooks and worksheets

When working in Excel, the files that you create and work with are called **workbooks**. Each workbook consists of a number of **worksheets** (the default number is three). You can add more worksheets to a workbook if necessary, or remove any that you don't need.

Related data is usually best kept on separate worksheets within the same workbook – this makes it easier to find and manage your data.

Worksheets

The worksheet tabs appear at the bottom left of your screen – to the left of the horizontal scrollbar.

To move from one sheet to another in your workbook:

  ♦   Click the sheet tab of the sheet you want to work on.

If you can't see all the sheet tabs in the bar, you can use the navigation buttons to the left of the sheet tabs to scroll the sheet tabs into view.

Add sheet

To insert a worksheet:

  ❶   Select the worksheet (click on the sheet tab) you want to have to the *right* of the new one.

  ❷   Open the **Insert** menu and choose **Worksheet**.

  ♦   A new worksheet will appear to the left of the selected one.

Delete sheet

If a workbook contains unwanted sheets you can easily delete them.

  ❶   Select the sheet you want to delete (click on the sheet tab).

  ❷   Open the **Edit** menu and choose **Delete Sheet**.

Be careful when deleting worksheets – Undo will not restore them!

Rename sheet

By default, worksheets are named Sheet1, Sheet2, etc. You can easily re-name the worksheets to give them a name that actually means something.

To rename a worksheet:

  ❶   Double click on the sheet tab you want to rename.

  ❷   Type in the name you want to use.

  ❸   Press [Enter] or click anywhere on the worksheet.

Move sheet

If you want to change the position of a worksheet within your workbook, you can drag it to the position required.

  ♦   Click and drag the worksheet tab of the sheet you want to move along the sheet tabs until it is in the correct place.

4.3 Spreadsheet jargon

Before going any further, spend a little time getting familiar with some of the jargon you will encounter. There's nothing difficult about it – once you know what it means!

Rows, columns and cells

The worksheet area consists of rows, columns and cells. Rows are identified by the numbers displayed down the left side of the worksheet area. Row 6 is highlighted in the illustration below. There are *lots* of rows on a worksheet – 65,536 in fact!

Columns are identified by letters displayed along the top of the worksheet area. Column C is highlighted in the illustration. After Z, columns are labelled AA to AZ, then BA to BZ, and so on to IV, giving 256 columns in all.

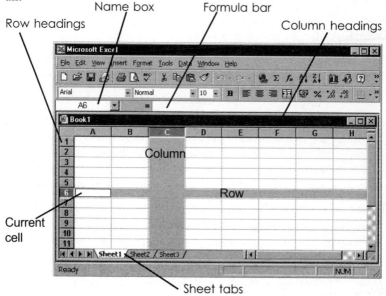

Where a row and column intersect you have a cell. Each of the rectangular areas on your worksheet is a cell. Cells are identified using a cell *name* or *address*. A cell address consists of the column letter followed by the row number of the column and row that intersect to create the cell.

Cell A1, B9, C3, D6 and F3 have been highlighted in this screenshot.

Text, data, formulas and functions

The cells in your worksheet will eventually contain text, numeric data, formulas or functions.

Text is used for titles or narrative to describe the figures – worksheet headings, column headings and row labels will usually be text entries.

Numeric data means the figures that appear in your worksheet. The data may be entered through the keyboard, or generated by a calculation.

Formulas are used to perform calculations on the data in your worksheet. Formulas are used to add the value in one cell to that in another or multiply the values in different cells, etc.

Functions are predefined formulas that perform simple or complex calculations on data. There are many different kinds of functions in Excel – statistical, logical, financial, database, engineering – and many more. You're bound to find useful ones, whatever type of data you work with.

4.4   Moving around your worksheet

Before you can enter anything into a cell, you must make the cell you want to work on active. To make a single cell active, you must select it. You can easily move onto any cell (thus making it active) using either the keyboard or the mouse.

The active cell has a dark border. The address of the active cell appears in the Name box to the left of the Formula bar.

Navigating with the mouse

♦ Scroll cell into view if necessary and click into it.

Navigating with the keyboard

To go to the next cell:

♦ Use the →, ←, ↑ and ↓ arrows on the keyboard.

To move onto the cell directly below:

♦ Press the [Enter] key.

To go to a specific cell address:

❶ Press the [F5] key on your keyboard.

❷ Enter the address of the cell in the **Reference** field of the **Go To** dialog box.

❸ Click **OK**.

To go to Cell A1:

♦ Press [Ctrl]-[Home].

To move to the end of your work area:

♦ Press [Ctrl]-[End].

Check out Keyboard shortcuts in the on-line Help to see if there are any others that you would find useful.

4.5 Selection techniques

You will find that you often work on more than one cell at a time in Excel. You may need to format a group of cells in a particular way or copy or move a group of cells, or apply a function to a group of cells.

A group of cells is called a cell *range*. Cell ranges are identified by using the first cell address followed by the last cell address in the group of cells you wish to work on, e.g. A1:A7, C3:D12, F5:H7 are highlighted in the screenshot on the next page.

You can *select* a cell range using either the mouse or the keyboard.

To select a group of adjacent cells:

- Click and drag.

To select a group of adjacent cells:

❶ Click on a cell in one corner of the range.

❷ Hold down [Shift] and click on the cell in the diagonally opposite corner of the range.

To select a row:

- Click the row number to the left of the row you want to select.

To select several adjacent rows:

- Click and drag down over the numbers to the left of the rows.

To select a column:

- Click the column letter at the top of the column.

To select several adjacent columns:

- Click and drag across the letters at the top of the columns.

To select the whole worksheet:

- Click the box at the top left of the row and column headers.

To select a range of *non*-adjacent cells:

❶ Click on one of the cells.

❷ Hold the [Ctrl] key down and click on each of other cells.

To de-select a range of cells:

- Click on any cell in your worksheet or press one of the arrow keys.

4.6 Entering text and numeric data

Entering text or data into your worksheet is easy.

❶ Select the cell you want to enter text or data into.

❷ Type in the text or data – the text or data will appear in the Formula bar as well as in the active cell.

❸ Press [Enter] or click the 'tick' button to the left of the formula bar when you've completed the cell.

Things to note when entering text:

♦ Text automatically aligns to the left of a cell.

♦ Text that doesn't fit into a single cell will 'spill over' into the cell to the right if it is empty.

♦ Excess text will not be displayed if the cell to the right is not empty. Widen the column (see 4.8) or reduce the font size to display it all.

Things to note when entering numeric data:

♦ Numeric data automatically aligns to the right of a cell.

♦ If a cell displays ######## instead of the figures you need to change the number format or adjust the column width to show all the data.

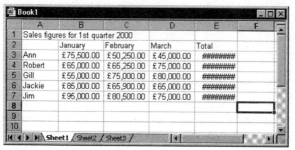

4.7 Editing text and numeric data

If you make an error when entering your work, you can fix things by deleting, replacing or editing the contents of the cell

To delete the contents of a cell (or cells):

❶ Select the cell(s) whose contents you want to erase.

❷ Press the [Delete] key.

To replace the contents of a cell:

❶ Select the cell whose contents you want to replace.

❷ Type in the text or data that should be in the cell.

To edit the contents of a cell:

❶ Select the cell whose contents you want to edit.

❷ Click in the formula bar to place the insertion point in it.

Or

♦ Double click in the cell whose contents you want to edit – this places the insertion point within the cell.

❸ Edit the cell contents as required.

❹ Press [Enter] when you've finished editing.

4.8 Column width/row height

All the columns in a worksheet are the same width unless you change them.

To change the width of a column manually:

♦ Drag the vertical line (in the column heading row) to the right of the column whose width you want to change, e.g. to change the width of column B drag the vertical line between column B and C.

To adjust the column width automatically:

♦ Double click the vertical line (in the column heading row) to the right of the column you want to adjust.

To change the height of a row manually:

♦ Click and drag the horizontal line (in the row heading) under the row whose height you want to adjust, e.g. to change the height of row 5 drag the horizontal line between row 5 and 6.

To adjust the row height automatically:

♦ Double click the horizontal line (in the row heading area) below the row you want to adjust.

You can also adjust the column width or row height from the **Format** menu.

4.9   Text wrap/shrink to fit/orientation

When entering text into cells you might want to try some other formatting options to help you display your work effectively. These options can be used on any cells, but may be particularly effective on column headings. Options include:

  ◆ Text wrap   ◆ Shrink to fit   ◆ Orientation   ◆ Vertical alignment

These options can all be found in the **Format Cells** dialog box, on the **Alignment** tab.

  ❶   Select the cells you want to format.
  ❷   Open the **Format** menu and choose **Cells...**
  ❸   Select the **Alignment** tab.
  ❹   Specify the option(s) required.
  ❺   Click **OK**.

  ◆   You may need to adjust the row height or column width manually
       if it doesn't adjust automatically to accommodate the alignment
       options you choose.

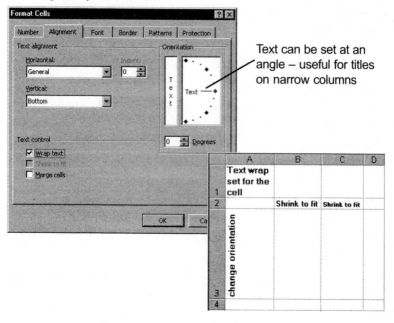

Text can be set at an angle – useful for titles on narrow columns

4.10 Number formats

A lot of the data entered into a worksheet is currency. Most of the times that you enter currency values, you will want the appropriate currency symbol to precede the figure.

If you want the £ symbol in front of a figure you can either:

♦   Format the cells to display the entry in a currency format.

Or

♦   Enter the £ symbol through the keyboard.

If you enter your figures through the numeric keypad, it's probably easiest to format the cells to display the figures as currency. You can format cells *before* or *after* you have entered your text or data.

To format the cells to display the figures in currency format:

❶   Select the cells you want to format.

❷   Click the **Currency** tool 🖳 on the Formatting toolbar.

The Formatting toolbar has other tools to help you format your numbers – Percent, Comma Style, Increase and Decrease Decimal. Other formats can be found in the **Format Cells** dialog box, on the **Number** tab – have a look to see if any would be useful to you.

To apply a format from the **Format Cells** dialog box:

❶   Select the cells you want to format.

❷   Open the **Format** menu and choose **Cells...**

❸   Select the **Number** tab.

❹   Choose a category from the list, e.g. Currency.

❺   Complete the dialog box as required, e.g. you may want to select a different symbol if the currency isn't '£'.

❻   Click **OK**.

4.11 Formulas

Any cell which will contain a figure that has been calculated using other data in your workbook, should have a formula in it (do *not* do your calculations on a calculator, then type the answer into your worksheet).

Formulas, using these arithmetic operators, allow you to add, subtract, divide, multiply and work out percentages of the values in cells.

+ Add   – Subtract   / Divide

* Multiply   % Percentage

Formula examples

=A7/B6   Divide the figure in A7 by the figure in B6

=D22*12   Multiply the figure in D22 by 12

=C7*25%   Calculate 25% of the figure in C7

Order of precedence

If there is a mixture of operators in a formula, Excel will deal with the multiplication and division *before* the addition and subtraction, e.g.

=A4+C7*D7   Multiply the figure in C7 by the one in D7, and add
                       the answer to the figure in A4

Parentheses

Some formulas can become quite long and complicated.

If you want to force the order in which a formula is worked out, or even just make a long formula easier to read, you must use parentheses ( ).

In the example below, the problem within each set of parentheses is solved *before* working through the formula

=((A1+B2)*C3)) – (D4/E5)

Add A1 to B2   we'll call this XX

Multiply XX by C3   we'll call this YY

Divide D4 by E5   we'll call this ZZ

Subtract ZZ from YY

4.12   AutoFill

AutoFill can be used to copy formulas down columns or across rows. In the screenshot, the formula in cell D4 is =B4–C4. We need a similar formula in the other cells in the column. To complete the cells using AutoFill:

❶   Select D4.

❷ Position the mouse pointer over the bottom right corner of the cell and the **Fill Handle** – a small black cross – should appear.

	A	B	C	D	E
1	Furniture Sale - everything reduced by 60%				
2					
3	Item	RRP	Sale Price	Saving	
4	Desk	£ 300.00	£ 120.00	£ 180.00	
5	Chair	£ 195.00	£ 78.00		
6	Table	£ 360.00	£ 144.00		
7	Bed	£ 400.00	£ 160.00		
8					

❸ Click and drag the black cross down over the other *Saving* cells.

When you let go the mouse, the formula in cell D4 will be copied to the cells you dragged over.

If you click on each cell in the *Saving* column and keep an eye on the Formula bar, you will notice that Excel has automatically changed the cell addresses in the formula *relative* to the position you have copied the formula to.

You can also use AutoFill to automatically generate days of the week, months of the year or dates.

❶ Enter January, Jan, Monday or Mon in any cell.

❷ AutoFill it down or across.

Dates

❶ Enter the first date in your series.

❷ AutoFill using the *right* mouse button.

❸ Select the Fill option required from the pop-up menu.

4.13 AutoSum

The worksheet opposite contains details of monthly sales figures.

To calculate the totals for each sales representative for the quarter, and the total for each month, we could use a formula, e.g. =B4+C4+D4, but the easiest and quickest way to calculate the total is to use *AutoSum*.

To calculate the totals using AutoSum:

❶ Select a cell in which you want a total figure to appear, e.g. E4 – the cell that will contain the total sales for the first sales person or the total for Quarter 1.

❷ Click the **AutoSum** tool Σ on the Standard toolbar.

	A	B	C	D	E	F
1	SALES FIGURES (1st Quarter 2000)					
2						
3		January	February	March	TOTAL	
4	Peter Johnston	£ 10,124	£ 12,452	£ 14,090		
5	Alison Kennedy	£ 12,400	£ 13,769	£ 15,089		
6	Diane Andrews	£ 9,670	£ 17,324	£ 12,400		
7	John Donaldson	£ 10,134	£ 12,908	£ 16,500		
8	Robert Burns	£ 11,340	£ 12,050	£ 14,000		
9	TOTAL					
10						

❸ The range of cells that are going to be added together will be highlighted. Note that the function also appears in the formula bar.

❹ If the suggested range of cells is correct, press [Enter].

Or

♦ If the suggested range is *not* the range of cells you want to add together, drag over the correct range, then press [Enter]. The total value of the selected range of cells will appear in the active cell.

♦ Use AutoFill to copy the function down or across the other *Total* cells.

If you are totalling rows and columns as in this example, you could use a shortcut that performs all the calculations in one move.

To AutoSum several groups of cells simultaneously:

❶ Select all of the rows and columns you want to total, and the cells that you want to contain the results of the AutoSum calculations.

❷ Click the **AutoSum** tool ∑ on the Standard toolbar.

The cells in the rightmost column and bottom row of the selected area will each have the Sum function inserted into them.

	A	B	C	D	E	F
1	SALES FIGURES (1st Quarter 2000)					
2						
3		January	February	March	TOTAL	
4	Peter Johnston	£ 10,124	£ 12,452	£ 14,090		
5	Alison Kennedy	£ 12,400	£ 13,769	£ 15,089		
6	Diane Andrews	£ 9,670	£ 17,324	£ 12,400		
7	John Donaldson	£ 10,134	£ 12,908	£ 16,500		
8	Robert Burns	£ 11,340	£ 12,050	£ 14,000		
9	TOTAL					
10						

Non-adjacent cells

You can also use AutoSum to total non-adjacent cells:

❶   Select the cell that will contain the result of the calculation.

❷   Click the **AutoSum** tool $\boxed{\Sigma}$ on the Standard toolbar.

❸   Click on the first cell you want to include in the range of cells.

❹   Hold the [Ctrl] key down and click on each of the other cells to be included in the formula.

❺   Press [Enter].

♦   If you prefer to type in the formula, you must start with an = (equals sign). A range of adjacent cells has the first cell address in the range entered, followed by a : (colon), then the last cell address in the range. The cell addresses for non-adjacent cells must be separated by a , (comma).

4.14   Insert and delete rows and columns

To add or delete rows or columns within worksheets try the following:

To insert a row:

❶   Select the row that will go *below* the row you are inserting.

❷   *Right* click within the selected area and choose **Insert** from the pop-up menu.

To insert a column:

❶   Select the column that will go to the right of the column you are inserting.

❷   *Right* click within the selected area and choose **Insert**.

To delete a row or column:

❶   Select the row or column you wish to delete.

❷   *Right* click within the selected area and choose **Delete**.

To add or delete several rows or columns at the same time:

❶   Click and drag in the row or column label area to indicate the number of rows or columns you want to insert or delete.

❷   *Right* click within the selected area and choose **Insert** or **Delete**.

4.15 Preview, page layout and print

At some stage you will want to print your file. Before sending a worksheet to print, it's a good idea to *preview* it.

Print Preview

You cannot edit an Excel worksheet in Print Preview. If you want to change something when you see the preview:

❶ Click the **Close** tool on the Print Preview toolbar to return to your worksheet.

❷ Edit the worksheet as required.

❸ Preview again to see how it looks.

You might want to change some of the page layout options to get the layout of your worksheet just as you want it. Some of the options are listed here.

Orientation

You can print a page either portrait (tall) or landscape (wide).

❶ From a worksheet, open the **File** menu and choose **Page Setup**.

Or

❷ If you are in **Print Preview**, click the **Setup…** button on the Print Preview toolbar.

❸ Select the **Page** tab.

❹ Choose the orientation option required.

❺ Click **OK**.

Scaling

If your worksheet is bigger than will fit on one sheet of paper, you can specify the number of pages that you want the worksheet to be print on to.

❶ Open the **File** menu.

❷ Choose **Page Setup**.

❸ Select the **Page** tab.

❹ In the Scaling options, specify the number of pages wide and the number of pages tall you want your worksheet to fit on.

❺ Click **OK**.

Page size

The default paper size is A4. You can change the page size if necessary.

❶ Open the **File** menu, choose **Page Setup** and select the **Page** tab.

❷ Choose the paper size required from the **Paper size** list.

❸ Click **OK**.

Margins

The margins are the space between the edge of your paper and your data.

❶ From the **File** menu, choose **Page Setup** and open the **Margins** tab.

❷ Specify the margins you want to use.

❸ Click **OK**.

Headers and footers

Headers and footers display information at the top or bottom of every page that prints out for your worksheet. You can format headers and footers from the **Custom Header...** or **Custom Footer...** dialog box.

❶ Open the **Page Setup** dialog box.

❷ Select the **Header/Footer** tab.

❸ Choose a header or footer from the lists and click **OK**.

Or

❹ Click **Custom Header...** or **Custom Footer...**

❺ Click in the section you want your header or footer to appear – left, centre or right.

❻ Type the text or click a button to add page numbers, date, time, etc.

❼ Select the text or field entered and format it as required (click the **Font** button – the first one in the dialog box).

❽ Click **OK**.

Print

When you are happy with the preview of your worksheet, you can send it to print.

If you are in print preview:

❶ Click **Print...** on the Print Preview toolbar.

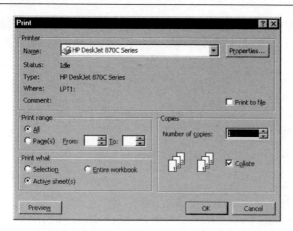

❷   Complete the **Print** dialog box as required – specify the **Print range, Copies** and **Print what** options as required.

❸   Click **OK**.

Print part of your worksheet

If you don't want to print all of your worksheet, you can print the area required on its own. To print part of your worksheet:

❶   Select the range of cells you want to print.

❷   Open the **File** menu and choose **Print...**

❸   Select *Selection* from the **Print what** options.

❹   Click **OK**.

4.16   Sort

The data in your worksheet can be sorted into ascending or descending order. You can perform a simple sort on the data, where you sort the data using the entries in one column only, or a more complex sort where you can sort on up to three columns at a time.

To perform a simple sort:

❶   Select any cell in the column you want to base your sort on.

❷   Click the **Sort Ascending** 　 or **Sort Descending** tool 　 on the Standard toolbar.

To perform a multi-level sort:

❶ Select any cell within the group of cells you want sorted.

❷ Open the **Data** menu and choose **Sort...**

❸ Select the main sort field from the **Sort by** list.

❹ Choose the order – ascending or descending.

❺ Select the second level sort field from the first **Then by** list, and set its sort order.

❻ If necessary, set the third level sort options.

❼ Click **OK**.

♦ Note that by default, Excel assumes your list has a Header row. The Header row is the row that normally contains the column labels or field names. If your list doesn't have a header row, i.e. you want the first row included in the sort, select the **No header row** option.

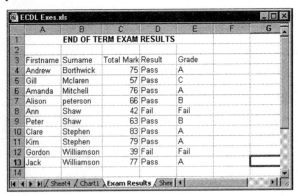

♦ The list in the example above has been sorted into Surname order (ascending) then Firstname order (ascending).

4.17   Formula Palette

This helps you enter your formulas and functions. Have a look at the Formula Palette – it makes the generation of formulas relatively easy!

♦   To display the Formula Palette, click the **Edit Formula** button (the = sign) to the left of the Formula bar.

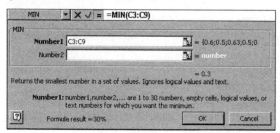

The most recently used function relating is displayed at the top of the function list, in the top left-hand corner of the palette.

♦   To change the function being used, click the drop down arrow to display the function list, and select a different function.

♦   If the Formula Palette obscures the area of the worksheet you want to view, click the button to the right of a data entry field – the palette will become minimized, so you can see your worksheet.

♦   To display the palette again, click the restore **Formula Palette** button at the right-hand side of the minimized window.

4.18   Statistical functions

These include minimum, maximum, average, count – and many others.

Minimum, Maximum, Average and Count

♦   To return the minimum value from a range use **MIN**.

♦   To return the maximum value from a range use **MAX**.

♦   To return the average value from a range use **AVERAGE**.

♦   To count the number of entries in a range use **COUNT**.

❶   Select the cell that the function will go in.

❷   Display the **Formula Palette**.

❸   Select the function from the function list, and jump to step 7.

Or

❹   Click **More Func-tions...** to display the **Paste Function** dialog box.

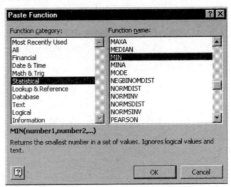

❺   Select a category from the **Function cat-egory** list.

◆   If the function you want has been used recently, it may be listed in the *Most Recently Used* set. If you're not sure what category the function you require is in, select the *All* category (every function is listed here, in alphabetical order). Minimum, Maximum, Average and Count can be found in the *Statistical* category.

❻   Scroll through the **Function name** list, select the function you re-quire and click **OK**.

❼   Enter the range of cells you want the function to operate on – either drag over the range on your worksheet, or enter the cell addresses through the keyboard (minimize the Formula Palette so you can see your worksheet if necessary).

❽   Restore the **Formula Palette** if necessary.

❾   Click **OK**.

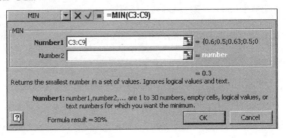

In this example statistical functions were used to display:

* The **lowest** mark in each exam (Minimum).

* The **highest** mark in each exam (Maximum).

* The **average** mark for each subject (Average).

* The **number** of students (Count).

	A	B	C	D	E
1	Exam Results				
2	Firstname	Surname	Maths	English	Computing
3	Alison	Anderson	60%	45%	80%
4	Bill	Andrews	50%	88%	59%
5	Gavin	Blair	63%	55%	72%
6	Jill	Blair	50%	80%	76%
7	Julie	Collins	74%	68%	78%
8	Paul	Dunsire	30%	60%	95%
9	Anne	Peterson	70%	68%	74%
10					
11	Lowest Mark		30%	45%	59%
12	Highest Mark		74%	88%	95%
13	Average Mark		57%	66%	76%
14					
15	Number of students		7		

4.19   View formula

When setting up your worksheet, it is sometimes useful to display and print the formulas that you have entered into the cells.

❶ Open the **Tools** menu and select **Options…**

❷ Select the **View** tab.

❸ Select (to show) or deselect (to hide) the **Formulas** checkbox.

❹ Click **OK**.

You may need to adjust the column widths to display the whole formula in some columns.

* You can print a copy of your worksheet out with the formulas displayed – you may find it useful for reference purposes.

The formulas used in the Exam Results worksheet are displayed here.

	A	B	C	D	E
1	Exam Results				
2	Firstname	Surname	Maths	English	Computing
3	Alison	Anderson	0.6	0.45	0.8
4	Bill	Andrews	0.5	0.88	0.59
5	Gavin	Blair	0.63	0.55	0.72
6	Jill	Blair	0.5	0.8	0.76
7	Julie	Collins	0.74	0.68	0.78
8	Paul	Dunsire	0.3	0.6	0.95
9	Anne	Peterson	0.7	0.68	0.74
10					
11	Lowest Mark		=MIN(C3:C9)	=MIN(D3:D9)	=MIN(E3:E9)
12	Highest Mark		=MAX(C3:C9)	=MAX(D3:D9)	=MAX(E3:E9)
13	Average Mark		=AVERAGE(C3:C9)	=AVERAGE(D3:D9)	=AVERAGE(E3:E9)
14					
15	Number of students		=COUNT(C3:C9)		

4.20   Relative and absolute cell addresses

You have already noticed that when you AutoFill or copy a formula, the cell addresses used in it change automatically, relative to the position you copy them to. By default, the cell addresses used are *relative addresses*.

There will be times when you use a cell address in a formula, and want to copy it down some rows or across some columns, but don't want the cell address to change relative to its new position.

In this example we have a list of products that we intend to sell in France. The prices are in £ but we want to convert them to francs so we can quote prices in the local currency for our customers.

The current exchange rate has been entered into cell B2. The formula to calculate the price of the first item in the list in francs (cell C5) will be =B5*B2. If you AutoFill the formula down the column, B5 needs to change to B6, B7 then B8 but we don't want B2 to change as each formula needs to pick up the rate of exchange figure.

To stop the cell address changing when it is copied, we must make it an *absolute address*. An absolute address will not change when the formula or function containing it is copied or moved.

	A	B	C	D
1	**Goods for export – France**			
2	**Rate of Exchange**	10.7	F/£	
3				
4	**Product**	**Price £**	**Price F**	
5	Bookcase	£ 350.00	3,745.00 F	
6	Bed	£ 475.00	5,082.50 F	
7	Chest of drawers	£ 250.00	2,675.00 F	
8	Coffee table	£ 175.00	1,872.50 F	
9				

To create an absolute cell address:

♦   Enter a $ sign in front of each coordinate you do not want to change – either type the $ sign, or press the [F4] key which will cycle through the possible combinations.

To absolutely address the cells in a formula:

❶   Select the cell that contains the formula (C5 in this example).

❷   Click in the **Formula** bar.

❸   Position the insertion point to the *right* of the cell address that you want to make absolute in the formula – B2.

❹   Press the [F4] key until you have the cell addressed properly.

♦   Each time you press the [F4] key it moves through the absolute addressing options. The formula should be =B5*B2.

B2   neither co-ordinate will change

B$2   the column will change if you copy the formula across columns

$B2   the row number will change if you copy the formula
         down rows

B2   both co-ordinates will change relative to the new position

❺   **AutoFill** the formula down the column.

4.21 Charts

Excel can create charts – bar graphs, line graphs, pie charts, scatter diagrams, etc. – from the data in your worksheet.

You can create your chart as an object on the same worksheet as the data on which the chart is built, or on a separate chart sheet.

- Data that you want to chart should *ideally* be in cells that are adjacent to each other.

- If the data you want to chart has blank rows or columns within it, remove these before you try to chart the data.

To chart data that is not in adjacent cells:

❶   Select the first group of cells you want to chart.

❷   Hold the [Ctrl] key down while you click and drag over the other groups you want to include in your chart.

- When non-adjacent cells are selected, the selected areas *must* form a rectangle.

	A	B	C	D	E	F	G
	ECDL Exes.xls						
1			BOOKSHOP SALE				
2							
3	Title	Rec Retail Price	Sale Price	Saving	No in Stock	Value of Stock	
4	Cats	£12.00	£ 4.80	£7.20	4	£ 19.20	
5	Wine tasting holidays	£14.00	£ 5.60	£8.40	6	£ 33.60	
6	Canal boat holidays	£10.00	£ 4.00	£6.00	12	£ 48.00	
7	Italian Family Cookbook	£14.50	£ 5.80	£8.70	8	£ 46.40	
8							
9			Total Value in Stock			£147.20	
10							

Sheet3 / Sheet4 / Chart1 / Exam Results \ S

Chart Wizard

This will step you through the process of setting up your chart.

❶   Select the data you want to chart – including the column headings and row labels.

❷   Click the **Chart Wizard** tool 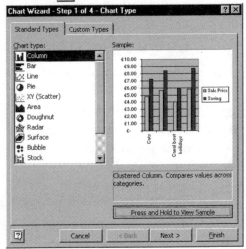 on the Standard toolbar.

❸   At step 1, select the **Chart type**.

*   Click the **Press and Hold to View Sample** button to see what your data would look like in your chosen type.

❹   Once you've decided on a type, click **Next**.

❺   At step 2, on the **Data Range** tab, check the data range selected, and decide whether you want to display the data series in rows or columns (try both and decide which you prefer). Click **Next**.

❻   At step 3, explore the tabs in the **Chart Options** dialog box and set the options you require. Click **Next** when you want to move on.

❼   Finally, decide where the chart should be located – in the worksheet, or on a separate Chart sheet. Click **Finish**.

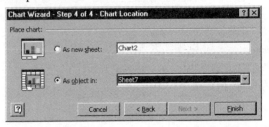

*   Any changes made to the data on which the chart is based will automatically be reflected in the chart, wherever it is located.

If you opt to insert your chart as an object in a worksheet, the Chart toolbar should be displayed when you return to the worksheet.

The chart will be selected – there will be *handles* in each corner and along each side. If you click on the worksheet area, the chart becomes de-selected, and the Chart toolbar disappears.

- ♦ To select the chart again, click on it once.

Chart objects

Each area of your chart is an object – you have a chart area object, plot area object, category axis object, value axis object, legend object, etc.

The chart must be selected (if it is an object in your workbook) before you can select the individual objects within it.

To select a chart object:

- ♦ Choose the object from the **Chart Objects** list .

Or

- ♦ Click on the object you want to select.

Move, resize and delete a chart in a worksheet

You can move, resize or delete a chart that is an object in your worksheet. To move the chart:

- ❶ Select the chart.
- ❷ Drag the chart to its new position.

To resize the chart:

- ❶ Select the chart.
- ❷ Point to one of the handles along the edge.
- ❸ Drag the handle to increase or decrease the size of the object.

To delete the chart:

- ❶ Select the chart.
- ❷ Press [Delete].

Formatting chart objects

To get the effect you want, you can change the formatting of each object in a chart, e.g. the colours in a bar chart, or the position of the legend.

To format an object in your chart:

♦   Double click the chart object you want to format.

When the **Format** dialog box appears, explore it to see the various formatting options you have.

Experiment with the options until you find the right formatting for your chart.

♦   If you want to format the font of an object, you can use the tools on the Formatting toolbar – font, font size, bold, italic, etc.

To change the chart type

If your chart doesn't look the way you expected, and you think a different chart type would be better, you can change the chart type at any time.

To change the chart type:

❶   Click the drop down arrow to the right of the **Chart Type** tool on the Chart toolbar.

❷   Select the type of chart required.

♦   The **Chart** menu appears when you have a chart selected or when you are on a Chart sheet. Take a look at the options in it.

Chart Type... displays the dialog box from Step 1 of the Wizard. You get access to all the chart types and sub-types from here.

Source Data... displays the dialog box from Step 2. If you need to edit the data range, this is the best place to do it.

Chart Options... displays the dialog box from Step 3. You can add titles, change the position of the legend, edit the gridlines, etc. through this box.

Location... displays the dialog box from Step 4. You can change the location of the selected chart from here – you can move it to another sheet, or put it on a Chart sheet.

A chart on a separate sheet

If you opt to locate your chart in a new sheet, your chart will be displayed on a sheet called *Chart1* (unless you've already got a *Chart1* sheet, in which case it will be in the *Chart2* sheet or *Chart3* sheet). The chart sheet is inserted to the left of the worksheet that its data is on.

The Chart toolbar should be displayed when the Chart sheet is selected.

You can use the Chart toolbar, or the **Format** or **Chart** menu to modify the chart as required.

You can rename the *Chart1* sheet name to something more meaningful, move the sheet to another location in your workbook, or delete the chart sheet if you decide you don't need it any more.

Printing your chart

You can print your chart with or without the data on which it is based.

To print a chart that is an object within your worksheet you have several options. I suggest you do a Print Preview before you actually print, just to check it looks okay.

To print out all of the data on the worksheet *and* the chart:

♦   Print the worksheet as normal (with the chart de-selected)

To get a print out of the chart only:

♦   Select the chart on the worksheet, then print.

To get the chart, plus the data on which it is based, but no other data from the worksheet:

❶   Select the chart.

❷   Click the **Data Table** tool 🔲 on the Chart toolbar to display the data table for the chart.

❸   Print out with the chart selected.

To print a chart that is on a separate Chart sheet:

❶   Select the Chart sheet.

❷   Print as usual.

♦   If you also want to print out the data on which the chart is based, display the Data Table before you print.

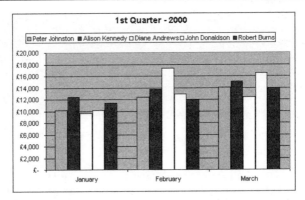

- You can use the drawing tools to create different effects on your worksheet data and charts. If you create charts, try using an Arrow and a Text Box to add emphasis to it! (8.12)

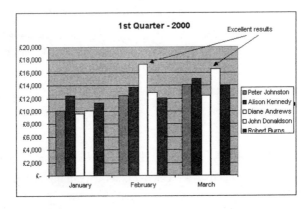

4.22   Mock test

Read *The tests* section in the Preface before you start.

Preparation

In the ECDL test the files will be provided on disk, but in order to practise, you could type the following data into Excel and save the workbook
as Expenses. (The errors in the headings are intentional!) Put the Sum
function (use AutoSum) in the cells in the total column and row.

Expenses							
Item	January	February	March	April	Maiy	June	Total
Flights							
Acommodation							
Meels							
Phone							
Other							

Save your files and close Excel before you try the mock test. Remember,
no notes (although you can use the on-line help if you need to), and no
more than 45 minutes for the whole test!

Test

In this test you will create a spreadsheet for the local primary school PTA.
You have been asked to prepare an outline cost plan for four events coming up over the new school year. You will also have to carry out various
formatting actions, and make some calculations before presenting the
spreadsheet to the next committee meeting. Each task is worth 1 mark,
except task 5 which is worth 4 marks. You must get at least 24/30 to pass.

1. Open the spreadsheet application.

2. Open the workbook *Expenses* from your disk and change the *header*
    (NOT heading!) to Arial point size 16.

3. Save the workbook *Expenses* in a template file format to your disk.

4. Close the workbook *Expenses*

5. Create a new workbook and set up the following budget using the

cell references as indicated in the table below. Leave the cells marked formula empty. No other formatting is required at this stage.

	A	B	C	D	E	F
1	PTA Events					
2						
3	Title	Catering	Music/ Entertainment	Venue Hire	Promotion Materials	Total Cost
4	Halloween Party	250	50	0	20	formula
5	Winter Fair	100	0	40	40	formula
6	Spring Music Festival	200	0	40	30	formula
7	Summer BBQ	1000	50	0	40	formula
8	Average	formula	formula	formula	formula	
9						

6. Select the budget title, *PTA Events, Cell A1*, and make the cell contents bold and size 14.

7. Delete the contents of *Cell B5*. Enter *300* as the new figure.

8. Insert a new row between rows 7 and 8, so that the Average figures will appear in row 9.

9. Create a formula to calculate the total cost for the Hallowe'en Party in *Cell F4*.

10. Use AutoFill to extend this formula down to *Cell F7*.

11. Create the formula to calculate the average amount spent on catering in *Cell B9*.

12. Use the AutoFill to extend this formula along to *Cell E9*.

13. Put borders around the whole table, excluding the header, and between each cell.

14. Format all figures in the spreadsheet to currency.

15. Format all column headings to allow text wrap within the cell.

16. In Row 9, *Average*, format the numbers to show no decimal places.

17. Add a header *Expenses Estimate* typed in the centre.

18. Save the workbook as *PTAEvents* and print two copies of it to a printer (if available) *or* to a print file.

    (N.B. – two copies will require two different filenames.)

19. Go to a new worksheet in the *PTAEvents* workbook (probably Sheet 2). Type *Data copied from PTA Events sheet* into *Cell A14*.

20. Copy all text and figures from the first sheet in the *PTAEvents* workbook to the new sheet at *Cell A1*.

21. Return to the first worksheet. Create a bar chart on this sheet (make the chart an object in the same worksheet as the data), from the data contained within *Title* and *Total Cost* columns for the different events.

22. Use *Costing for proposed events* as a title for the chart.

23. Make each bar in the bar chart a different colour e.g. yellow, green, black, etc.

24. Place the legend at the top of the chart.

25. Adjust the document so that the data table and the chart will appear on the same page when printed. You are not going to print the document. Save your workbook.

26. Open the workbook called *Expenses*. Use a spell-check program and make any changes where necessary.

27. Save all your workbooks and close the spreadsheet program.

SUMMARY

This chapter has covered the material required for Module 4, Spreadsheets. You have learnt about:

✓ Worksheets and workbooks.

✓ Entering text and data into a worksheet.

✓ Adjusting column widths and row heights.

✓ Formatting options that are specific to spreadsheets.

✓ Entering formulas using the operators +, -, * and /.

✓ The Sum function.

✓ AutoFill.

✓ Statistical functions – Average, Minimum, Maximum, Count.

✓ Absolute addressing.

✓ Sorting your data.

✓ Creating and manipulating charts.

5 | DATABASES

AIMS OF THIS CHAPTER

This chapter uses Microsoft Access to introduce you to databases. You will learn how to create a database – name fields, specify data types, set properties, set the primary key, etc. You will learn how to input and edit data in a table and a form. You will also learn how to extract records from your database using specific criteria. Finally, you will find out how to produce a simple report. In this chapter I have suggested a database that you can set up – by all means set up your own database to practise on if you prefer.

5.1 Planning and design

A simple database could be used to record name and address details (e.g. your Christmas card list). You could also use a database to store and manage details of your CD collection, or to organize the data you need to run your company (supplier, customer, stock, order details, etc.).

In a simple database, it may be feasible to store all the information together in one table – perhaps with a Christmas card name and address list. Other databases are more complex with several tables, e.g. the video store database set up in this chapter.

Database jargon

Some database terminology may be unfamiliar to you. Here are brief definitions of the terms you are likely to encounter in the near future.

In a relational database, all the data on one topic is stored in a **table**. In a simple database, you might have only one table. More complex databases may consist of several tables.

A **record** contains information about a single item in your table. All the detail relating to one video will be held in that video's record in the Video table.

A **field** is a piece of data within a record, e.g. in a video's record, things like video code, title, classification and rental price.

Relationships determine the way in which the detail in one table is related to the detail in another table, e.g. through the video code.

Joining is the process of linking tables or queries.

Data definition is the process of defining what data will be stored in your database, specifying the data field's type (number, text, currency), the data field's size and indicating how it is related to data in other tables.

Once your data is set up, you can work with it in many ways through **data manipulation** – this may involve sorting it into a specific order, extracting specific records from tables, or listing detail from a number of different tables into one report.

- Each *record* in a table is presented in a *row*.
- Each *field* in a record is in a *column*.
- Each field has a *field name* at the top of the column.

The diagram opposite illustrates a simple database.

Access objects

An Access database consists of **objects** that can be used to input, display, interrogate, print and automate your work. These objects are listed in the **Database** window. The objects that you will use are summarized below:

Tables are the most important objects in your database. Tables are used for data entry and edit.

You use **queries** to locate specific records within your tables.

You can use **forms** to provide an alternative to tables for data entry and viewing records.

Reports can be used to produce printed output from data in the database.

VIDEO STORE DATABASE

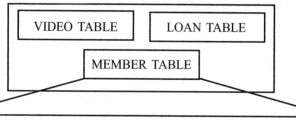

MEMBERS TABLE					
Member-ship No	Title	First Name	Last Name	Address	Telephone No
1	Mr	Joe	Simpson	10 High St	0131 555 1111
2	Miss	Angela	Armstrong	14 St. Stephen St	0131 111 1000
3	Mr	Brian	Wilson	14 Johnston Cres	0131 000 1111
4	Mrs	Karen	Andrews	122 Main St	0131 333 1111

Preparing your data

Before you set up a database you should decide:

♦   What data do you want to store? (members' names/addresses, video titles, etc.)

♦   What information do you want to get out of your database? (a list of all videos that are overdue, in a particular classification, etc.)

If you work out the answers to these questions, you will be in a position to start working out what fields you need.

If you are setting up names, you would probably break the name into three fields – *Title*, *First name* (or *Initials*) and *Last name*. This way you can sort the file into Last name order, or search for someone using the First name and Last name.

If you are storing addresses, you would probably want separate fields for *Address/Street*, *Town/City*, *Region* and/or *Country*. You can then sort your records into order on any of these fields, or locate records by specifying appropriate search criteria. For example, using *Address/Street* and *Town/City* fields, you could search for people who live in St John's Street (Address/Street), Stirling (Town/City) rather than St John's Street, Dundee.

When planning your database, take a sample of the data you wish to store and examine it carefully. This will help to confirm what fields are needed.

How big are the fields?

You must decide how much space is required for each field – it must be long enough to accommodate the longest item that might go there. How long is the longest last name you want to store? If in doubt, take a sample of some typical names (Anderson, Johnston, Mackenzie, Harvey-Jones?) and add a few more characters to the longest one to be sure.

Minimize duplication

Try to group your fields into tables with a view to minimizing the duplication of data in your database. There are several benefits to this approach:

♦ Each set of details is stored (and therefore keyed in) only once.

♦ The tables end up smaller than they otherwise might have been.

♦ As you don't have much duplication of data, the database is easier to maintain and keep up to date.

It is very important that you spend time organizing and structuring your data before you start to computerize it – it'll save you a lot of time and frustration in the long run!

5.2 Starting Access

When you start Access, the Access copyright screen will appear on your screen for a few seconds, followed by the **Microsoft Access** dialog box.

♦ Choose **Blank Access database** and click **OK**.

You then arrive at the **File New Database** dialog box.

You must now decide where you want to store your database (My Documents is the default).

As with all Microsoft packages, a temporary filename is suggested for your database – in Access these follow the pattern *db1*, *db2*, *db3* in

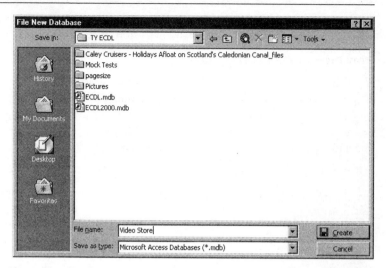

each working session. You should replace the temporary name with a name that means something to you and reflects the contents of your database.

In this chapter you can imagine you are running a video store. You are setting up a database so that you can record details of:

♦ videos that you have in your store

♦ the names and addresses of your members

♦ who has what on hire and when it is due back.

Name your database *Video Store*.

♦ Once you have named your database click the **Create** button.

This takes you through into Access, with your Video Store database window displayed. You are ready to start setting up your database.

5.3 The Access screen

You should be able to identify the following areas within the Access application window:

♦ Title bar   ♦ Menu bar   ♦ Status bar

♦ Database toolbar   ♦ Database window

♦ Minimize, Maximize/Restore and Close buttons

Application Title bar   Application Minimize, Maximize/
                                              Restore, Close buttons
    Database Title Bar

            Database toolbar

                Database window toolbar

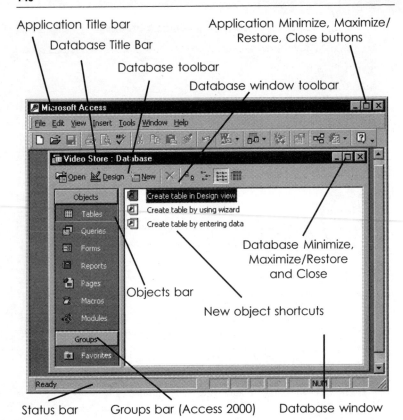

Status bar   Groups bar (Access 2000)   Database window

Within the **Database** window we have the:

- Title Bar   • Objects bar   • Database window toolbar
- Minimize, Maximize/Restore and Close buttons
- New object shortcuts   • Groups bar (Access 2000)

These areas will be referred to often during the course of this book, and in any other publications you read.

5.4 Creating a new Database

If you are already in Access, but have not yet created the Video Store database file, do so now:

❶ Click the **New** tool ▣ on the Database toolbar.

❷ At the **New** dialog box, choose **Database** from the **General** tab.

❸ Click **OK**.

❹ Specify the folder you wish to save your database into.

❺ Give the database a name.

❻ Click **Create**.

5.5 Field data types and properties

There are ten different data types to choose from when setting up your table structures. Brief notes on each type are given below for your information. Most of your fields will probably be Text, with a few of the others used in each table depending on the type of data you wish to store.

Data type	Usage	Size	Notes
Text	Alphanumeric data	up to 255 bytes	Default data type
Memo	Alphanumeric data – paragraphs	up to 64,000 bytes	Cannot be indexed For notes and comments
Number	Numeric data	1,2,4 or 8 bytes	
Date	Dates and times	8 bytes	Date and time values for the years 100 through to 9999
Currency	Monetary data	8 bytes	Can be used for calculations on numbers with up to four decimal places. Accurate to 15 significant figures
Auto Number	Unique long integer generated by Access for each new record	4 bytes	Cannot be updated Useful for Primary Key fields
Yes/No	Boolean data	1 bit	Fields that hold one of two values – Yes/No, On/Off, True/False. Displayed as a checkbox at data entry stage
OLE Object	Pictures, graphs or other objects from another Windows application	Up to 1 gigabyte	Cannot be indexed

Data type	Usage	Size	Notes
Lookup	Creates a field that allows you to look up values in another table or from a list using a combo box. Choosing this data type starts the Lookup Wizard	Typically 4 bytes	It is the same size as the Primary Key used to perform the lookup
Hyperlink	Inserts a 'hot spot' that lets you jump to another location on your computer, on your intranet or the Internet	The address can contain up to four parts (each part can be up to 2048 characters)	The four parts are: Text to display* Address Subaddress* Screentip * optional

You can customize each field by specifying different properties. The properties vary depending on the data type you choose. The various properties you will encounter are listed here:

Property	Data Type	Notes
Field Size	Text and Number data types Number field sizes are: Byte (single byte) Integer (2-byte) Long Integer (4-byte) Single (4-byte) Double (8-byte)	Text fields from1–255 (default 50) Values: $0 - 255$ $-32,768$ to $32,767$ $-2,147,483,648$ to $2,147,483,648$ -3.4×10^{38} to 3.4×10^{38} -1.797×10^{308} to $+1.797 \times 10^{308}$
Format		You can control how your data is displayed or printed. The options available vary with the data type
Decimal Places	For number and currency data types	Choose from Auto (two decimal places for most formats, but with *General*, it displays the number of places required by the precision of the number), or a fixed display (0 through to 15 decimal places)

Property	Data Type	Notes
Input Mask	For Text, Number, Currency and Date/Time data types	When setting up a pattern, you use special characters to show the type of input allowed, and whether or not input is required
Caption		A more descriptive field name that displays on forms and reports
Default	All except AutoNumber, Memo and OLE Object	
Validation Rule		An expression that must be true when data is entered or edited
Validation Text		The message to appear on screen when a validation rule is not met
Required		The field must be completed
Allow Zero Length	Text and Memo fields	
Indexed	Text, Number, Date/Time, Currency and AutoNumber	Indexing speeds up access to the data values. Index fields that will be sorted or queried on
Unicode Compression	Text, Memo and Hyperlink	Worldwide character encoding standard. Leave at default –Yes

5.6 Creating a new table

❶ Select **Tables** on the Objects bar.

❷ Click ⊞New on the Database window toolbar.

❸ Select **Design View**.

❹ Click **OK**.

In Design view you can specify the field names, data types and any other properties you think would be useful.

The tables that you set up in your database must have a structure or design. In the table design you identify the fields required, their data types and any other properties that are important.

We will set up three table designs in our database:

* Video table
* Member table
* Loan table.

We could set up a more sophisticated database for this application, with additional tables where data could be 'looked up' for some fields, but that is beyond the scope of what is required for your ECDL certificate.

Defining the Video table

The Video table will contain the fields listed below.

Field Name	Data Type	Properties
VideoID	AutoNumber	Primary Key
Title	Text	Field Size = 25, Indexed
Classification	Text	Field Size = 20
Year released	Text	Field Size = 4
Company	Text	Field Size = 30
Rental price	Currency	

Our first field is the *VideoID*.

❶ In the **Field Name** column, key in the field name – *VideoID*.

❷ Press [Tab] to move along to the **Data Type** column and set this to **AutoNumber** (click the drop down arrow to display the options). Access will complete this field automatically during data entry.

❸ Press [Tab] to move along to the **Description** column and enter a field description if you wish.

* The Description is optional – anything you key in the description column will appear on the status bar during data entry to that field.

The Design view window has two panes – an upper one where you specify the field name, data type and description, and a lower one where you specify the field properties.

* To move from column to column in the upper pane, press [Tab].
* To move from one pane to the other press [F6] (once you've entered some data in the upper pane).
* You can point and click with the mouse to move around the window.

Primary Key

The *VideoID* field is the primary key for this table – each video has a unique code – its unique identifier.

◆ To establish Primary Key status, click the Primary Key tool 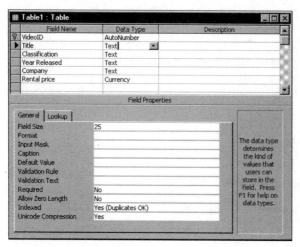 when the insertion point is anywhere in the *VideoID* field row in the upper pane.

Note that the Index property is automatically set to YES (No Duplicates) when a field is given Primary Key status.

Enter the Video title details in the second row of the upper pane.

❶ In the **Field Name** column, key in the field name – *Title*.

❷ Press the [Tab] key to move along to the **Data Type** column and set this to *Text*.

◆ The default field size for a Text data type is 50 characters. This is more than is required for a video title, so this property could be reduced – 25 would be big enough.

❸ Press [F6] to move to the lower pane (or click with the mouse) and change the field size from 50 to 25.

❹ Set the **Indexed property** to *Yes (Duplicates OK)*.

Enter the remaining fields following the suggestions in the table on page 144.

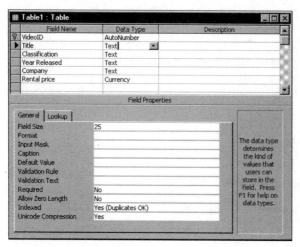

To Save and Close the table design window:

❶   Click the **Save** tool  on the Table Design toolbar.

❷   Give your table a suitable
     name, e.g. *Video*.

❸   Click **OK**.

❹   Close the **Table Design**
     window.

Your new table will be listed under Tables in the **Database** window.

Setting up the Member table

Field Name	Data Type	Properties	Notes
MemberID	AutoNumber		Primary Key
Title	Text	Field size = 6	
First name/Initial	Text	Field size = 20	
Surname	Text	Field size = 25	Indexed (Duplicates OK)
Address	Text	Field size = 30	
Town	Text	Field size = 20	Indexed (Duplicates OK)
Postcode	Text	Field size = 10	
Region	Text	Field size = 20	Indexed (Duplicates OK)
Telephone No	Text	Field size = 12	
Child Member	Yes/No		

❶   Select **Tables** on the Objects bar in the **Database** window.

❷   Click **New**.

❸   At the **New Table** dialog box, select **Design View**.

❹   Click **OK**.

◆   Set up the structure for this table, following the suggestions above.

◆   Save and close the table.

Defining the Loan table

The Loan table is set up in a similar way. Set up the design for the Loan table following these guidelines.

Field Name	Data Type	Properties
MemberID	Number	Long Integer
VideoID	Number	Long Integer
Return Date	Date/Time	Short Date
Paid	Yes/No	

◆ Save the Loan table and close the **Table Design** window.

DO NOT set a Primary Key for this table – any field in it may end up having a duplicate value as you enter details of who has hired what.

5.7 Relationships

We now have to set up the relationships between these tables.

❶ Click the **Relationships** tool 🔲 on the Database toolbar at the **Database** window. The **Relationships** window opens.

◆ The **Show Table** window should also be open – if it isn't click the **Show Table** tool 🔲 to display a list of the tables in your database.

❷ Select the table (or tables) you wish to add to the **Relationships** window and click the **Add** button.

◆ You can add several tables at the same time if you wish.

◆ If the tables are listed next to each other in the **Show Table** dialog box, select the first table you wish to add, then point to the last table, hold down [Shift] and click – all the tables within the range will be selected.

◆ If the tables you wish to select are not next to each other, click on the first one you want to select, then hold down [Ctrl] while you click on each of the other tables required.

❸ Click the **Close** button once you have added your tables.

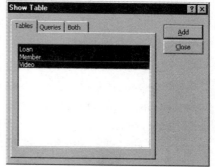

We need to create two relationships, one between the Member table and Loan table using the MemberID field, and one between the Video table and Loan table using the VideoID field. With the tables related, we will be able to pull information from more than one table at a time if necessary (later in this chapter).

To create a relationship:

❶ Click on the field you wish to relate to another table to select it.

❷ Drag the selected field and drop it onto the field you wish to link it to in the other table.

❸ At the **Edit Relationships** dialog box, click **Create** to establish the relationship.

❹ Click **OK**.

The lines running between the tables are called *Join Lines*. The Join Lines run between the fields linking the tables. Access will often create the link between tables automatically – especially if there are fields with the same name in different tables. Access will assume that where two tables have the same field name in them, these fields are the ones that link the tables.

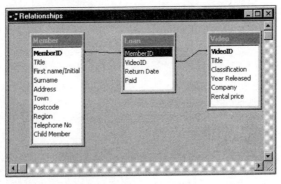

To delete an existing relationship:

❶ Click on the Join Line you wish to remove to select it.

❷ Press the [Delete] key on your keyboard.

❸ Respond to the prompt as required.

• Save the changes made to the Relationship window if you wish to keep them and close the Relationship window when you have finished working with it.

5.8 Entering data in Datasheet View

You should have the Video Store database open. The three tables will be listed in the Tables area of the **Database** window.

Data entry is very easy for the most part – simply open the table and key in the data. As you are keying in, look out for the features mentioned below.

* To open a table in Datasheet view, double click on the table name, or select the table required in the **Tables** list and click **Open**.

In Datasheet view, your table looks similar to a spreadsheet layout – each record is presented in a row and each field is in a column.

* To move forward through the fields press [Tab].
* To move backward through the fields press [Shift]-[Tab].
* Or click in the field you want to move to using the mouse.

Video table

AutoNumber

* The *VideoID* field has the AutoNumber data type. This field is completed automatically by Access – you cannot enter data into it.

❶ Enter the following video details (add more records if you wish).

	VideoID	Title	Class	Year Rel	Company	Rental price	
⊞	1	Matilda	PG	1996	TriStar Pictures	£2.00	
⊞	2	Friends - Series 4	12	1998	Warner Bros	£2.00	
⊞	3	Dad's Army - The Movie	U	1971	Columbia	£1.00	
⊞	4	Fawlty Towers	PG	1994	BBC	£1.50	
⊞	5	Good Morning Vietnam	15		Touchstone	£1.50	
⊞	6	Babe	U	1995	Universal	£2.00	
▶	(AutoN)					£0.00	

Record: ⏮ ◀ ☐ 7 ▶ ⏭ ▶* of 7

❷ Close the table when you've finished entering your data (you don't need to save your data, Access does this automatically).

Member table

❶ Enter ten records into this table. Make them up!

* Notice that the *Child Member (Yes/No)* datatype appears as a checkbox. A tick in the box means yes, an empty box means no.

❷ Close the table when you've finished.

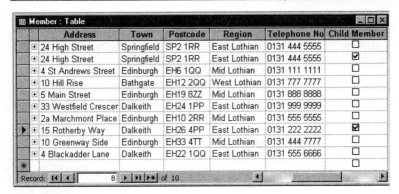

Loan table

❶   Enter details of a few loans currently out – you need a *VideoID*,
     MemberID (both of which must exist in the other tables) and the
     return date for each video.

❷   Close the table when you've finished.

5.9   Datasheet and Design View

If you discover a problem with your table design, you can move from
Datasheet view to Design view to fix it. To go to Design view:

◆   Click the **View** tool 📝 on the Table Datasheet toolbar.

If you make any changes to the design of your table, you must remember
to save them. Be careful not to make any design changes that will result in
you losing data that you need, e.g. reducing the size of a field too much.

To move back into Datasheet view:

◆   Click the **View** tool 📰 on the Table Design toolbar.

5.10   Editing data in Datasheet View

Moving through your table

We have already discussed the fact that you can move within and between
records using the [Tab], [Shift]-[Tab] keyboard techniques, or by pointing
and clicking in the desired field using the mouse.

At the bottom left of the table window, you will find a set of navigation buttons that you can use to move through your table in Datasheet view.

* The record number field tells you which record the insertion point is currently in, and to the right of this you will find the total number of records in your table.

Editing the field contents

If you spot an error in Datasheet view, position the insertion point within the field you wish to edit, and make whatever changes are required.

You can use the scroll bars (horizontal and vertical), or the navigation buttons to locate the record you need to update. Once the record has been located, the simplest technique is to click within the field that needs to be changed and insert or delete data as necessary.

If you use [Tab] or [Shift]-[Tab] to move through fields that contain data, the contents of a field are selected when you move on to it.

* To replace the selected data within a field, simply key in the new text – whatever you key in will replace the original data.

* To delete the data in the field press [Delete] when the data is still selected.

* To add or delete data without removing the current contents of the field, you must deselect the field contents before you edit.

To deselect the field contents, either click within the field, or press [F2]. Once the data is deselected you can position the insertion point and insert or delete as required.

Add record

❶ Click the **New Record** tool ▸* on the Table Datasheet toolbar.

❷ Enter your record details into the empty row.

Delete record

❶ Place the insertion point within the record you wish to delete.

❷ Click the **Delete Record** tool ✗ on the Table Datasheet toolbar.

5.11   Formatting options in Datasheet View

If you don't like the formatting options on your datasheet, try something else. The Font, Cell Format and Row height options described below are applied to the whole table – you don't need to select anything first.

Font

❶   Choose **Font...** from the **Format** menu.

❷   Complete the dialog box with details of the font style, size and attributes required.

❸   Click **OK**.

Cell Format

❶   Choose **Datasheet...** from the **Format** menu.

❷   Specify which gridlines you wish to show, the gridline colour, the background colour and cell effect required.

❸   Click **OK**.

Row height

❶   Choose **Row Height...** from the **Format** menu.

❷   Specify a row height, or select the **Standard Height** checkbox.

❸   Click **OK**.

Column width

❶   Place the insertion point anywhere within the column.

❷   Choose **Column Width...** from the **Format** menu.

❸   Specify the width required or select **Standard Width** and click **OK**.

Or

♦   Let Access work out the best size by choosing **Best Fit**.

5.12   AutoForm

As an alternative to entering data into a table in Datasheet view, you could use Form view.

In Datasheet view, each record is displayed in a row, each field in a column. As many fields and records are displayed in the table window as will fit.

In Form view, the fields are arranged attractively on the screen (you can design forms to resemble paper forms you actually use) and one record is displayed at a time. Form view is often considered more 'user friendly' than Datasheet view.

Access has a useful tool that builds a simple form automatically – AutoForm.

- Try it out by creating forms for your Member and Video tables.

AutoForm from the Database Window

To create an AutoForm for a table:

❶ Select the table from the Tables list in the **Database** window.

❷ On the Database toolbar, click the drop down arrow to the right of the **New Object** tool.

❸ Choose **AutoForm**.

The table you selected is displayed using a simple form layout, or form with a subform (as in this example).

You can move around in Form view in the same way as in Datasheet view:

- Press [Tab] or [Shift]-[Tab] to move from field to field, or click in the field you want input or edit.

- Use the navigation buttons to move from record to record, or to the first or last record in the table.

- To go to a specific record, type in the record number field, the number of the record you wish to go to and press [Enter].

- Click the new record button to get a blank form on which to enter new data.

- If necessary, use the scroll bars to display parts of the form that are not displayed in the window.

The data you enter or edit in your form in Form view will be stored in the table on which the form is based. Even if you opt not to save the form itself, the data will still be stored in the table.

AutoForm from Datasheet View

If you have been working on your table in Datasheet view, you can easily change to Form view using the AutoForm tool.

In Datasheet view, there is also a **New Object** tool on the Table Datasheet toolbar. Choose AutoForm from the drop down list to display your datasheet in Form view.

Changing Views

When working with a form, you have three views of your table to choose from – Design, Datasheet and Form. To change views:

❶ Click the drop down arrow to the right of the **View** tool.

❷ Click on the view required.

The design of your AutoForm can be edited in Forms Design view – you can move the fields, resize them, change the labels, delete fields, etc.

5.13   Form Design

The layout of a form is set up in Form Design view. If you set a form up from scratch (without using AutoForm), you will work in Form Design view. You can also edit the layout of any form created using AutoForm in Form Design view.

In this section we will discuss editing a form created using AutoForm in Form Design view. To take your form from Form view into Design view:

❶ Choose **Design View** from the View options.

- The Form Design window will appear on your screen. The form on page 153 looks like this in Form Design view.

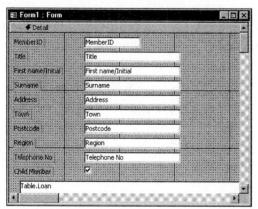

- The Form is designed on a grid.
- The Field List (displaying the field names from the table on which you are building the form) and the Toolbox (used to add labels, lines, etc. to your form) may also be displayed.
- ❷ Click the **Field List** tool 🗐 to toggle the display of the Field List.
- ❸ Click the **Toolbox** tool 🛠 to toggle the display of the Toolbox.

Form areas

The main areas in a form are the:

- Detail area
- Form Header and Footer area
- Page Header and Footer area.

The **Detail area** is present on every form. It is the part of your form in which most of the detail from your table will be displayed.

The **Form Header and Footer areas** appear above and below the detail area for each record when the form is in Form view. Form Headers and Footers are used for titles or instructions you wish to appear on each form. These areas are optional. To toggle their display on and off:

- ❶ Open the **View** menu.
- ❷ Choose **Form Header/Footer**.

The **Page Headers and Footers** appear at the top and bottom of each page, should you opt to print your form out. These areas are also optional. To toggle their display on and off:

❶   Open the **View** menu.

❷   Choose **Page Header/Footer**.

If you enter any data into the Form or Page Header or Footer area, then opt *not* to display the area, the data you entered will be lost.

The form on page 155 could be modified by adding a heading (in the Form Header area) containing the text 'Member's Details'. The text 'Member's Details' would be placed in a *label.*

Labels are used for instructions or headings – in fact any text that doesn't come from the underlying table.

To add the text:

❶   Display the **Form Header and Footer** areas (see above).

❷   Click the **Label** tool [Aa] in the Toolbox.

❸   Move the mouse pointer into the form header area (notice the mouse pointer shape +A).

❹   Click in the form header area where you want your heading to go.

❺   Key in your heading.

❻   Click anywhere outside the label field.

♦   You can resize the form header or footer area by clicking and dragging the bottom edge of it (the mouse pointer will change to a black double-headed arrow when you are in the correct place).

Working with objects

The objects (fields, labels, etc.) on your form can be moved, resized, formatted or deleted, so it's not critical that you get everything right first time.

To edit an object:

♦   Select the object – click on it.

♦   You will notice that a selected field has 'handles' around it – one in each corner and one half way along each side.

To resize:

♦ Click and drag a handle in the direction you wish to resize the field.

To move a field:

♦ Point to the edge of the field (not a handle) and drag – the pointer looks like a hand when you are in the correct place.

To delete a field:

♦ Select it, then press [Delete].

♦ To change the formatting, use the tools on the Formatting (Form/Report) toolbar.

♦ If you want your form to be wider, click and drag its rightmost edge to resize it.

Background colour

To change the background colour of your form:

❶ Select the area you wish to format – detail, header, footer, etc.

❷ Click the drop down arrow beside the **Fill/Back color** options.

❸ Choose a colour.

Saving your form

If you want to save your form, click the **Save** tool on the Form Design toolbar. At the **Save As** dialog box, either accept the default form name, or edit it as required, and click **OK**.

If you close your form without first saving it, Access will ask you if you want to save the form.

♦ **Yes** will take you to the **Save As** dialog box.

+ **No** will close the form without saving it.
+ **Cancel** will return you to Form Design view.

If you save your form, it will be listed under **Forms** in the **Database** window. You can open the form again from this list at any time – either double click on the form name or select the form name and click **Open**.

5.14 Changing the table structure

To edit the table structure you must take your table into Design view. You can do this from the **Database** window if you select the table you need to edit on the **Tables** tab, and click **Design**. If you are already in Datasheet view, you can go into Design view by clicking the **Table View** tool.

Adding a new field

+ If the new field is to go at the end of the structure, scroll through the rows until you reach the empty row under the existing fields. Enter the field name, data type and properties as required.

To add a new field between two existing fields:

❶ Place the insertion point in the upper pane anywhere within the field that will be below your new field.

❷ Click the **Insert Rows** tool ⊞ – a new empty row is inserted above the one the insertion point is in.

❸ Enter the field name, data type, etc as required.

Deleting a field

❶ Place the insertion point in the upper pane within the field.

❷ Click the **Delete Rows** tool ⊞.

❸ Respond to the prompt – choose **Yes** to delete the field.

Be careful when deleting a field – any data held within it will be lost.

Changing the field properties

❶ Place the insertion point in the upper pane within the field.

❷ Press [F6] to move to the lower pane.

❸ Edit the properties as required.

❹ Press [F6] to return to the upper pane.

When changing a field size, watch that you don't end up losing data. If you reduce the field size, any record that has data in that field in excess of the new field size will have the extra characters chopped off!

Primary Key

To change the field that has Primary Key status:

❶ Place the insertion point within the field in the upper pane that you want to take Primary Key status.

❷ Click the **Primary Key** tool 🔑 .

To remove Primary Key status, and not give it to any other field:

❶ Place the insertion point within the field in the upper pane that currently has Primary Key status.

❷ Click the **Primary Key** tool.

Renaming a field

You can rename a field in either Design view or in Datasheet view.

To rename a field in Design view:

♦ Edit the name in the first column in the upper pane.

To rename a field in Datasheet view:

❶ Double click on the field name in the **Field Name** row.

❷ Edit the field name as required.

❸ Press [Enter] or click in the record detail area.

5.15   Rearranging the fields

You can move the fields in either Design view or Datasheet view.

Design View

❶ In the upper pane, click in the row selector bar to the left of the field.

❷ With the pointer over the selector bar area, drag and drop the field into its new position – you will notice a thick dark horizontal line that indicates the position that the field will move to.

To keep the fields in their new position you must save the design before you close your table.

Datasheet View

❶   Select the field by clicking in the **Field Name** row above the field you wish to move.

❷   With the pointer in the **Field Name** row, drag and drop the field into its new position – a thick dark vertical line that indicates the position that the field will move to.

When you close your table, you will be asked if you wish to save the layout changes to your table. Respond **Yes** (to save) or **No** (to close the table without saving) or **Cancel** (to return to the table to do more work).

5.16   Printing your tables

You can print the contents of your tables from Datasheet view or from the **Database** window (simply select the table you want to print before you click the Print tool). See section 8.11 for details on Preview and Print.

5.17   Margins and orientation

If you need to change the margins, or the orientation of your table before you print it, go into the Page Setup options. To view the options:

❶   Open your table in Datasheet view.

❷   Select **Page Setup...** from the **File** menu.

♦   On the **Margins** tab, you can change the top, bottom, left or right margins. You can also specify whether or not you want to print the field name (column headings) at the top of each field.

♦   On the **Page** tab, you can change the orientation (portrait or land-scape), the paper size and source details, and the printer details.

5.18   Sort

Simple sort

❶   Open the table you are going to sort.

❷   Place the insertion point anywhere within the field you want to sort the records on.

❸   Click the **Sort Ascending** ⬆ or **Sort Descending** ⬇ tool.

When you close a table that you have sorted, you will be asked if you want to save the changes.

To save the records in the new, sorted order, choose Yes, if you don't want to save the changes, choose No.

Multi level sort

If you want to sort your table on several fields, you must set up your sort requirements in the **Filter** dialog box.

You could sort your Member Table into ascending order on Surname, and then by First name. If necessary, open your Member Table to try this out.

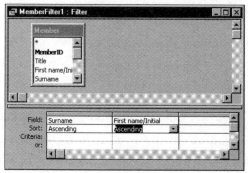

❶ Open the **Records** menu and select **Filter, Advanced Filter/Sort…**

✦ In the upper half of the **Filter** dialog box is the field list of the current table. Scroll through the list until you see your main sort field.

❷ Double click on the field name required – it will appear in the first row, first column of the query grid.

❸ Select the sort options in the **Sort Row** below the field name.

❹ Return to the upper pane and double click on the field required for your second level sort.

❺ Once you have set up the options, click the **Apply Filter** tool ▽ on the Filter/Sort toolbar to display your records in the new order.

You can save the options you have set up as a Query. You must return to the **Filter** dialog box to do this (Records, Filter, Advanced Filter/Sort…).

❶ Click the **Save As Query** tool 🔳 on the Filter/Sort toolbar.

❷   Give your query a suitable name.

❸   Click **OK**.

Your query will be listed under Queries in the **Database** window.

5.19   Find

To locate a record in your table, you can use the navigation buttons, or the record number field in the navigation buttons.

You can also locate records using Find:

❶   In Datasheet view, place the insertion point within the field that contains the text you want to find.

❷   Click the **Find** tool on the Table Datasheet toolbar.

❸   Enter details of what you are looking for in the **Find What** field.

❹   Edit the other fields as necessary.

❺   Click **Find Next** to find the first matching record.

❻   If it is not the record you want, click **Find Next** until you reach the correct record.

❼   Close the dialog box once you have found your record.

If Access can't find what you are looking for, a dialog box will tell you that the search string wasn't found. If this happens, check your entry in the Find What fields carefully – you may have typed it in incorrectly.

5.20   Filter

There may be times when you want to display a specific group of records from your table. This can be done by 'filtering' the records. You can filter your records 'By Selection' or 'By Form'.

Filter By Selection

❶   Open the table in Datasheet view if necessary.

❷   Position the insertion point in the field of a record that has the criteria you are looking for.

❸   Click the **Filter By Selection** tool . A subset of the records within your table will be displayed.

- You can filter your filtered list using the same technique – narrowing down your list of records as you go.

- To show all the records again, click the **Remove Filter** ▽ tool.

Filter By Form

When you Filter By Form, you can specify multiple criteria at the one time (unlike Filter By Selection where you narrow down your search one criteria at a time).

❶ Click the **Filter By Form** tool 🗐.

- You are presented with an empty record.

As you move from field to field, you will notice that each field behaves like a Combo Box in which you can display a list of options to choose from.

❷ Select the filter criteria using the drop down lists.

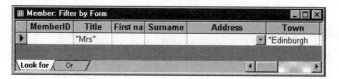

❸ Click the **Apply Filter** tool ▽ – all records meeting the criteria will be displayed.

❹ You can display all your records by clicking **Remove Filter** ▽.

5.21 Querying multiple tables

There may be times when you need to collect data from several tables, and sort or filter that data. When working across several tables, you must set up a Query from the Database window. In this example a query is used to produce a list of each member's name, the name of the video they have hired, and the date it is due back.

Start from the Database window.

❶ Select **Queries** in the Objects bar and click **New** 🗐 New on the **Database** window toolbar.

❷ At the **New Query** dialog box, choose **Design View** and click **OK**.

❸ You will arrive at the **Select Query** window. The **Show Table** window should be open, listing the tables in your database. If it is not open, click the **Show Table** tool 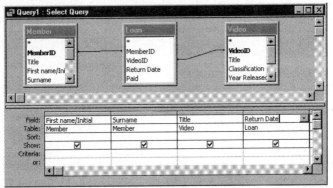 to display it.

❹ Add the tables you need to the **Select Query** window – all three in this example.

❺ Close the **Show Table** window.

There are some extra rows in the lower pane of the **Select Query** window.

◆ The Table row displays the name of the table from which a field is taken.

◆ The Show row indicates whether or not a selected field will be displayed in the result – a tick in the box means the field detail will be displayed, no tick means the detail will not be displayed. The default for all fields is that the detail will be displayed.

❻ Select the fields you want, in the order you want them to appear.

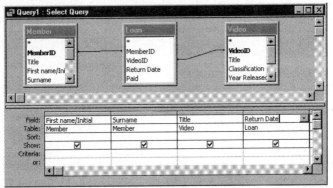

❼ Run your query – click the **Run** tool on the Query Design toolbar. A list of members and the videos they have hired out will be displayed. Save your query if you want to reuse it.

❽ Close your Query.

Specifying criteria

The criteria are specified through expressions that you key into the criteria rows in the query grid. When entering expressions note that:

- When you enter criteria in different cells in the same criteria row, Access uses the **And** operator. It looks for all the conditions being met before returning the record details.

- If you enter criteria in different cells in different criteria rows, Access uses the **Or** operator.

To specify a range of values, use the operators in your expressions.

<	Less than	>	Greater than
<=	Less than or equal to	=	Equal to
>=	Greater than or equal to	<>	Not equal to
Between...And...			

E.g. to list members who don't live in either Edinburgh or Dalkeith:

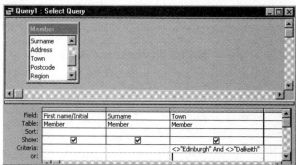

To get a list of Child Members only:

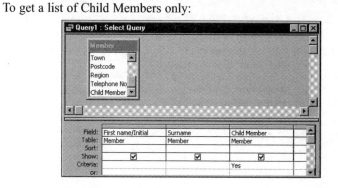

♦ Experiment with different criteria using your tables.

5.22 AutoReport

You can quickly design a simple report from any of your tables or queries using the AutoReport object. The report produced is a simple, single column report, listing all the fields in each record of the table or query.

To create an AutoReport from an open table or query:

❶ Display the **New Object** list.

❷ Select **AutoReport**.

♦ A simple report will be created using the data in the table or query you have open.

❸ When you close your report you will be asked if you want to save it. If you save it, the report will be listed under **Reports** in the **Database** window.

You do not need to open a table or query before you can create an AutoReport from it – you can do so from the **Database** window.

To generate an AutoReport from the **Database** window:

❶ Select the table or query you want to base your report on.

❷ Choose **AutoReport** from the New Object list.

Reports are displayed in Print Preview – so you can see what your page would look like if you were to print it out.

You can use the navigation buttons at the bottom of the Print Preview window to move through the pages in your report.

♦ Click the **View** tool on the Print Preview toolbar to take your report through into Design view.

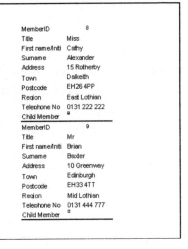

5.23 Report Design

The Design view of a report looks very similar to the Design view of a form.

The main areas in a report are the:

♦ Detail area

♦ Page header and footer area

♦ Report header and footer area.

The commands to switch the Page and/or Report Header and Footer areas on and off are in the View menu.

♦ The page header and footer area are displayed by default in an AutoReport design.

The field list, containing the field names from the table or query on which the report is based, is displayed – you can toggle the display of this by clicking the **Field List** tool ▣.

Page header and footer

Page headers are often used for column headings, or the report title, page footers are usually used for page numbering.

♦ You can easily add a page header using the **Label** tool 𝘼𝘢. You used the **Label** tool in Form design to add headings, instructions and other text to your form. The same techniques are used in Report design.

In the page footer area of a report, the page number is usually shown. The page number is placed in a Text Box.

❶ If necessary, scroll down through your form until you see the Page Footer area.

❷ Click the **Text Box** tool � then click and drag in the Page Footer area to indicate the position of the Text Box.

♦ A Text Box field consists of a description (the left part) and a detail area (the right part).

❸ Delete the description (left) part of the text box – select it and press the [Delete] key.

To get Access to put a page number in the Text Box:

❶   Select the box – click on it once .

❷   Type =**[Page]** in the field   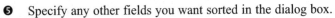 =[Page]   .

Grouping

You can easily group records in a report. You could group your members under the town that they live in. This is set up in the **Sorting And Grouping** dialog box.

❶   Click the **Sorting And Grouping** tool [≣] on the Report Design
        toolbar.

❷   Set the **Field/Expression**
        field – select the field to
        group on from the drop down
        list – *Town* in this example.

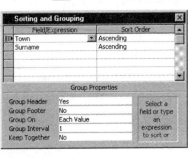

❸   Set the **Sort Order**.

❹   In the **Group Properties**
        pane set the **Group Header**
        property to *Yes* (so we can put
        the name of the town at the top of each group).

❺   Specify any other fields you want sorted in the dialog box.

❻   Close the dialog box to return to your design grid.

Move the *Town* field to the
group header area and re-
arrange the other fields as
required.

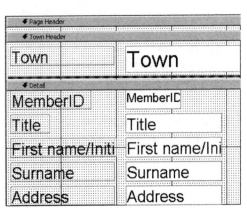

5.24   Finishing touches

By using the Toolbox and the Formatting toolbar, you can add the finishing touches to the objects in your report (or form) by adding lines, borders, colour and special effects.

To add a border:

❶   Click the **Rectangle** tool ⬚ on the Toolbox.

❷   Click and drag over the **Town Header** area – to draw a border around the label and detail parts.

♦   When you let go the button, the label and detail area are hidden. This is because they are under the rectangle you have just drawn. You must send the rectangle behind the text you want to show.

❸   Select the rectangle if you have deselected it.

❹   Open the **Format** menu.

❺   Choose **Send to Back**. The rectangle is sent behind the label and detail area and your label and detail area should be visible.

If you want top and bottom borders only, use the **Line** tool ◨ instead of the **Rectangle** tool. Drag to draw your lines wherever you want them.

You can change the line colour, thickness and add other effects to your border. Select the rectangle and experiment with the following tools to create different effects:

♦   Change the border colour using the **Line/Border Color** tool ◨.

♦   Change the border thickness with the **Line/Border Width** tool ◨.

♦   Select a new background colour with the **Fill/Back Color** tool ◨.

♦   Create a special effect with the **Special Effect** tool ◨.

Remember to save your report.

You'll probably find yourself jumping between Print Preview and Design View quite a lot until you get your report layout as you want it.

Print out your report (see 8.11) and close it.

♦   Close your database when you've finished work on it.

5.25   Mock tests

Read *The tests* section in the Preface before you start. In the ECDL test the files will be provided on disk, but in order to practise, you could type and save the database below. This test is in two parts, each part is worth 15 marks, giving a total of 30. You must score at least 24/30 to pass.

Preparation

Create a database called *ECDLMock* before you start. Create a new table called *Books* and enter the data on page 171. Set appropriate data types, and enter the data exactly as shown. Close the database and Access before you attempt the test. This file will be used in part 2 of the mock test.

In the first part of the test you will be asked to create a database, design a table, enter some records and produce a simple form that could be used for data entry. You should give careful consideration to the data types and field sizes used when setting up the structure of your table.

Test Part 1

1. Open the database application and create a new database called *Personnel*.

2. Design a table with five fields using the appropriate data types, distinguishing between text, numeric, date, etc., and with appropriate field sizes.

   ♦ The following fields must be created:
   EmployeeID
   Name
   Date of Birth
   Department
   Salary

3. Save your table as *Employees*.

4. Enter two complete records in your new database. Print the table.

5. Sort the table by *Name* (ascending order). Print the results.

6. Create a simple form to input data.

7. Save the form as *Employee Form*

8. Add a header to the form with the words *Employee Details*.

ISBN	Title	Author	Publisher	Year	Category	Price
014 032382 3	In & Out Stories	Andrew Watson	Hodder & Stoughton	1987	Children	£3.99
015 056473 6	Teach Yourself Access 2000	Moira Stephen	Hodder & Stoughton	2000	Computing	£8.99
0345 12342 3	Campfire Cooking	Ann Collins	Wilson-Simpson	1995	Cooking	£4.99
034532 375 1	Garden Shrubs	Trudy Veitch	Henderson	1986	Gardening	£4.99
0412 32132 2	African Drums	Bunty Simpson	Poodle	1992	Adult Fiction	£12.50
0465 77654 3	Giant World Atlas	Gerald Ferguson	Dollins	1991	Geography	£35.00
055345 456 2	The Night Sky	Jack Yooung	Rainbow	1991	Astronomy	£35.00
0563 49124 5	Bread and Biscuits	Alex Anderson	BCC	1987	Cooking	£12.50
0587 39561 0	Changing Skies	Louise Baxter	Henderson	1990	Astronomy	£10.99
0758 34512 1	Perfect Pizzas	Alison Simpson	BCC	1986	Cooking	£15.00
099988 452 1	The Tortoise in the Corner	Coral Baxter	BCC	1991	Children	£6.50

9. Enter one more record using the form for data entry.

10. Save the form and close it. Print the *Employees* table again. Close the Database.

Test Part 2

In the second part of the test you will be asked to query an existing database (if you have set up the **ECDLMock** database, use it for practice). You will be asked to perform a series of tasks on this data to demonstrate your ability to query a table and design a simple report.

1. Open the *ECDLMock* database and open the *Books* table.

2. Find the record for the author whose surname is *Yooung*.

- This name has been entered incorrectly, change it to *Young*.

3. Create a query to extract all records for all the books published by BCC – include all the fields from the *Books* table in your query.

4. Save your query as *BCC*. Run the query and print the results.

5. Change the query to produce only the *Author*, *Title* and *Publisher* of each book (for all publishers).

6. Sort the query in ascending sequence of *Title*.

7. Save the query as *Title*. Run the query and print the results. Close the query.

8. Produce a report from the *Books* table showing all the information sorted by *Title*. Save the report as *Title Report*. Print the report and close it.

9. Create a new query and extract all records of books that cost more than £10.

- Sort the data in ascending order on *Price*.

- Include the fields *Title*, *Publisher* and *Price*.

- Save the query as *PRICE*. Run the query and print the results.

10. Save all files.

11. Close the application.

SUMMARY

This chapter has discussed setting up and manipulating a database using Microsoft Access. Topics covered included:

- ✓ Planning and designing a database.
- ✓ Database jargon and Access objects.
- ✓ Data types and properties.
- ✓ Primary Key.
- ✓ Setting up and editing the table design.
- ✓ Entering and editing data.
- ✓ Relationships.
- ✓ Formatting the datasheet.
- ✓ Printing the datasheet.
- ✓ AutoForm.
- ✓ Form Design view.
- ✓ Sorting data – on single and multiple fields.
- ✓ Using Find to locate records.
- ✓ Extracting records using the Filter option.
- ✓ Setting up and running a simple Query.
- ✓ AutoReport.
- ✓ Report Design view.

6 | PRESENTATIONS

AIMS OF THIS CHAPTER

This chapter discusses PowerPoint, a presentation graphics package. You will learn how to create slides, make notes, prepare handouts and give a presentation. The topics discussed will prepare you for the ECDL Module 6 test.

I suggest you set up a presentation to practise on – choose a hobby that interests you or any topic you are familiar with.

6.1 Introduction to PowerPoint

PowerPoint is a presentation graphics package. You can use it to produce:

Slides

Slides are the individual pages of your presentation. They may contain text, graphs, clip art, tables, drawings and animation, video clips, visuals created in other applications, shapes – and more!! You can present your slides via a slide show on your computer, 35mm slides or overhead projector transparencies.

Notes pages

A speaker's notes page accompanies each slide you create. Each notes page contains a small image of the slide plus any notes you type in. You can print the pages and use them to prompt you during your presentation.

Handouts

Handouts consist of smaller, printed versions of your slides that can be printed two, three or six slides to a page. They provide useful backup material for your audience and can easily be customized with your company name or logo.

Outline

Your presentation Outline contains the slide titles and main text items, but neither art nor text typed in using the text tool. The Outline gives a useful overview of your presentation's structure.

6.2 Getting started

When you open PowerPoint you arrive at the **PowerPoint** dialog box, where you start to set up your Presentation.

The options for creating a new presentation are:

- ◆ AutoContent Wizard
- ◆ Design Template
- ◆ Blank presentation.

You can also choose:

- ◆ Open an existing presentation.

The last option takes you to the **Open** dialog box, where you can open an existing presentation.

The PowerPoint window is very similar to the other Office application windows.

The Standard and Formatting toolbars usually appear along the top of the window.

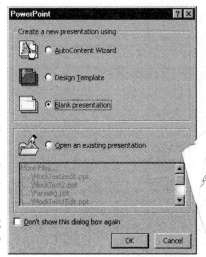

The Drawing Toolbar is usually along the bottom of the window.

PowerPoint objects

The text and graphics that you can place on a slide in PowerPoint are called **objects**. Objects that you can use include: text, tables, drawings, sounds, WordArt, graphs, Organization Charts or movies.

Toolbars

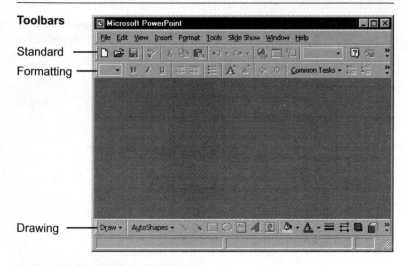

Standard

Formatting

Drawing

6.3 Creating a new presentation

From the **PowerPoint** dialog box:

AutoContent Wizard

Use this option if you want to start by using a wizard that helps you work out the content and organization of your presentation.

Design Template

This options lets you pick a presentation template with the colour scheme, fonts and other design features already set up.

❶ At the **PowerPoint** dialog box select the **Design Template** option.

❷ Click ᴏᴋ.

❸ Choose the Presentation design you wish to use from the Design Templates, Office 95 Templates or Office 97 Templates tabs in the **New Presentation** dialog box.

❹ Click ᴏᴋ.

❺ Select a slide layout at the **New Slide** dialog box – usually the Title slide for the first slide in your presentation.

❻ Click ᴏᴋ.

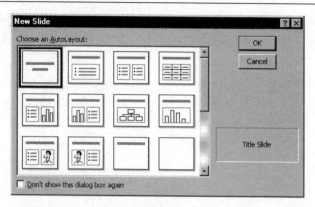

Once PowerPoint has set up your presentation, it displays it in Normal View. The first slide is displayed, ready for your input.

Blank presentation

If you opt for this one, you get a blank presentation with the colour scheme, font and design features set to the default values.

❶ At the **PowerPoint** dialog box select the **Blank** presentation option.

❷ Click [OK].

❸ Choose a slide layout for your first slide – usually the Title Slide.

❹ Click [OK].

♦ The boxes with broken outlines that appear when you create a new slide are called *placeholders*. Different slide layouts have different placeholders set up – the placeholders will contain the slide title, slide text and any other objects that you display on your slide.

Alternatively, to create a new blank presentation from within PowerPoint:

♦ Click 🗋 on the Standard toolbar. Select the slide layout required for the first slide from the **New Slide** dialog box and click [OK].

6.4 View options

By default, PowerPoint displays all new presentations in Normal view (PowerPoint 2000). You can use the view icons ▣▤▢▦▭ at the bottom left of the screen to get a different view of your presentation.

You will do most of the work setting up your presentation in Normal, Outline or Slide view – it's very much a matter of personal preference.

Outline   Slide

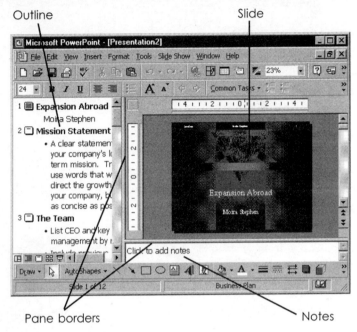

Pane borders   Notes

In Normal, Outline and Slide view, you have three panes displaying different parts of your presentation. The slide itself is in the top right pane, notes are displayed in the bottom right pane and an outline of your presentation is displayed in the left pane.

◆   You can resize the panes if you wish – click and drag the pane border to do so.

You can also view your presentation in Slide Sorter view and Slide Show view.

In Slide Sorter view each slide is displayed in miniature – this view can be used for moving slides around and to help you prepare for the actual presentation.

◆   You can also go into Slide Show view at any time to see how your slide will look in the final presentation. Press [Esc] from Slide Show view to return to your presentation file.

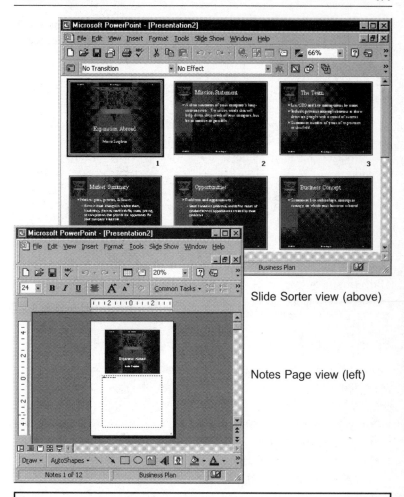

Slide Sorter view (above)

Notes Page view (left)

THE VIEW MENU

You can also change views using the View menu. The View menu lists a view option called Notes Page view. This view displays a miniature of your slide, with the notes area displayed below it. You can also enter and edit your notes in this view. If you wish to do this use the **Zoom** tool on the Standard toolbar to zoom into about 75% so that you can read the text.

◆   I suggest you use Normal view for the most part – I think you'll find it the best compromise. Try out the others and see what you think – my personal preference is Normal.

6.5 Working with slides

Once you've created your presentation using one of the methods discussed, the next step is to decide on the text that you want to appear on your slides – the title, and the main points that you want to discuss during your presentation.

The main text on a slide will be in the slide title or the bulleted list area.

You can determine the structure of the text on each slide (main points, sub-points, etc.), using up to five levels if necessary.

```
┌─────────────────────────────────────┐
│            Slide Title               │
│  Level 1                             │
│        Level 2                       │
│            Level 3                   │
│                Level 4               │
│                    Level 5           │
└─────────────────────────────────────┘
```

Entering text

To enter text onto a new slide, e.g. the title slide created when setting up a presentation using the Design Template or Blank Presentation option, follow the prompts, e.g.:

❶   Click in the *Title* area.

❷   Key in your text.

❸   Click in the bulleted list area.

❹   Key in your text and press [Enter].

❺   Repeat step 4 until all your points are listed.

◆   If you have created a presentation using the AutoContent Wizard, select the text on each slide and replace it with the text you wish to use.

Editing text

❶   Locate the slide you want to edit.

❷   Click to place the insertion point inside the text to be edited.

❸   Insert or delete characters as required.

♦   If you want to change the text completely, select the old text (click and drag over it) and key in the replacement text.

Moving between slides

In the slide pane, you see one slide at a time on your screen. If you have several slides, you must move up or down through them to view them.

❶   Drag the elevator (the 'box' on the scrollbar) up or down the scroll bar to the desired slide.

♦   Note the slide number that appears when you drag the elevator. When you let go the mouse button, the slide indicated appears on the screen.

Or

❷   Click the **Previous Slide** button to move up a slide at a time (at the bottom of the vertical scroll bar).

❸   Click the **Next Slide** button to move down a slide at a time.

♦   You can also move back to the previous slide using [Page Up], or on to the next using [Page Down].

Adding new slides

You can add new slides at any place in your presentation (not just at the end).

❶   View the slide that you want *above* your new one.

❷   Click the **New Slide** tool ⊟ on the Standard toolbar (*not* the New tool).

❸   Select a layout.

❹   Click ▐ OK ▐.

Promoting and demoting

The points you want to make on your slides will be structured – you will have main points (at the first bulleted level) and some of these points may have sub-points (at the second, third, fourth or even fifth level).

Initially, all points on your slide are at level 1. You can easily demote sub-items if necessary (and promote them again if you change your mind).

❶   Place the insertion point in the item.

To demote an item:

◆   Click the **Demote** tool ⬛ on the Formatting (or Outlining) toolbar.

To promote an item:

◆   Click the **Promote** tool ⬛ on the Formatting (or Outlining) toolbar.

Moving bullet points

You can easily rearrange the points on your slide using cut and paste or drag and drop techniques, or click inside the item you wish to move and press [Shift]-[Alt]-⬆ to move it up, [Shift]-[Alt]-⬇ to move it down.

Moving and deleting slides

To move slides:

❶   In the **Outline** pane, click on the icon to the left of the slide.

❷   Use cut and paste to move the slide to its new location.

Or

❸   In **Slide Sorter** view, drag and drop the miniatures to move slides.

To delete slides:

❶   In the **Outline** pane (in Outline or Normal view), click the slide icon on the left of the title to select the slide.

❷   Press the [Delete] key.

◆   With the insertion point in the slide pane, choose Delete Slide from the Edit menu.

6.6   Formatting

Most of the formatting options, e.g. bold, alignment and bullets work in the same way as in all other applications. Formatting options that are unique to PowerPoint include:

Changing a slide layout

If you decide you have chosen the wrong layout for a slide, it is easily changed.

❶   View the slide whose layout you wish to change.

❷   Click the **Slide Layout** tool 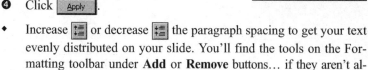 on the Standard toolbar.

Or

♦   Choose **Slide Layout** from the **Common
    Tasks** list on the Formatting toolbar.

❸   Select the Layout you want to use.

❹   Click **Apply**.

♦   Increase ⊞ or decrease ⊟ the paragraph spacing to get your text
    evenly distributed on your slide. You'll find the tools on the For-
    matting toolbar under **Add** or **Remove** buttons… if they aren't al-
    ready on the toolbar. Select the paragraphs first!

Changing the template

You can change your presentation template at any time. The template de-
termines the design elements of your presentation – colour, fonts, alignment of text, etc.

❶   Double click the template name field on the Status bar.

Or

♦   Choose **Apply Design Template…** from the Common Tasks list .

❷   Select the Template you want to use.

❸   Click **Apply**.

Background styles

When you select a template for your presentation, the slide background
colour and shading are picked up from the options set in the template. You
can easily change the colour and shading options while still retaining the
other design elements of the template.

If your presentation were in sections, e.g. on individual departments, or
regional figures, you could set a different background colour for each section of your presentation.

❶   Display the slide you want to change the background colour of.

❷   Choose **Background…** from the **Format** menu.

❸   Choose the **Background Fill** option required from the list.

❹ Click **More Colors...** and/or **Fill Effects...**, if required, select from the dialog boxes and click **OK**.

❺ Click 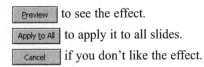 to apply it to the selected slide.

Or

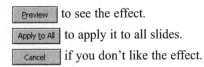 to see the effect.

 to apply it to all slides.

 if you don't like the effect.

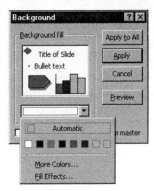

And yet more options...

Experiment with the various dialog boxes to see what effects are available.

You can select several slides at once in Slide Sorter view then change the colours of them all in one operation.

◆   To select several adjacent slides in Slide Sorter view, click on the first one, then [Shift]-click on the last one you wish to select.

◆   To select non-adjacent cells, click on the first one, then hold the [Ctrl] key down while you click on each of the others.

6.7   Headers and footers

If you want to add slide numbers, the date, time or any other header or footer to your slide, notes or handouts use the Header and Footer command.

❶ Open the **View** menu.

❷ Choose **Header and Footer...**.

❸ Select the appropriate tab – Slide or Notes and Handouts.

❹ Tick the items you want to appear, giving details as needed.

❺ Click [Apply] or [Apply to All].

6.8 Charts

Charts can be useful if you have figures to present but feel that a graphical representation would be more effective than the figures themselves.

- ◆ Add a slide that has a Chart placeholder.
- ❶ Double click within the Chart placeholder to move into the graph environment.

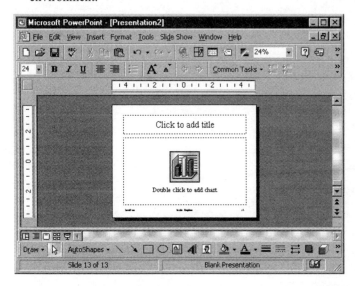

Datasheet and toolbars

The graphical environment has its own Standard and Formatting toolbars. There is also a small **Datasheet** window (which can be moved or resized as necessary), where you can key in the data you want to chart.

Standard toolbar

Formatting toolbar

Entering your own data

You must replace the sample data in the datasheet with the data you want to chart. If you do not need to replace all the sample data, delete the cell contents that are not required – select the cell and press [Delete].

▦ Presentation2 - Datasheet		A	B	C	D	▲
		1st Qtr	2nd Qtr	3rd Qtr	4th Qtr	
1 ▥▦	East	20.4	27.4	90	20.4	
2 ▥▦	West	30.6	38.6	34.6	31.6	
3 ▥▦	North	45.9	46.9	45	43.9	
4						▼

❶ Select the cell into which you wish to enter your own data.

❷ Key in the data.

❸ Move to the next cell you want to work on.

◆ Don't enter too much data – the chart will be seen on a slide, PC screen or overhead. If it's too detailed your audience may not fully appreciate it.

Moving around your datasheet

There are a number of ways to move from cell to cell within the Datasheet window. You can use:

Arrow keys	to move one cell in the direction of the arrow
[Tab]	to go forward to the next cell
[Shift]-[Tab]	to go back to the previous cell
[Enter]	to go down to the next cell in a column

Or

◆ Point to the cell and click.

The selected cell (your *current* cell) has a dark border.

View/hide datasheet

Once you have keyed in your data, you can hide the datasheet so you can see the chart clearly on your screen. If you hide it, you can easily view it again if you need to edit any data.

◆ Click the **View Datasheet** tool ▦ on the Standard toolbar to view or hide the Datasheet, as required.

By Row and By Column

◆ The *Category* axis has labels taken from the column or row head-ings in your datasheet. Use the **By Row** and **By Column** tools on the Standard toolbar to indicate whether your data series is in rows or columns. A graphic in the row or column heading of your datasheet indicates the selected option.

Chart type

The default chart type is a column chart. You can try out a variety of other chart types using the **Chart Type** tool on the Standard toolbar.

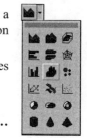

❶ Click the drop down arrow to display the chart types available.

❷ Choose one.

◆ Open the **Chart** menu and choose **Chart Type...** You'll find lots of other options to choose from.

Hiding columns

If you don't want all your data to be displayed on your chart, you can hide rows or columns as required. This is done on the datasheet.

❶ Display the datasheet if necessary.

❷ Double click on the heading of the column or row you wish to hide.

◆ The data is dimmed, and is not displayed on your chart.

❸ Double click the heading again to unhide the column or row.

◆ Use the **Text Box** and **Arrow** tools on the Drawing toolbar to add emphasis to your charts.

Colours and patterns

If you don't like the colour of a data series – the bars representing one set of data on your chart – try experimenting with the options available.

To change the colour of a whole data series:

❶ With the chart selected, double click on an item (e.g. bar or line) in the data series you want to format.

❷ On the **Patterns** tab of the **Format Data Series** dialog box select the options required.

❸ If you want a pattern, click **Fill Effects...**

❹ **Experiment** with the Fill Effects until you find something you like.

❺ Click ⟨ OK ⟩ then ⟨ OK ⟩ again to exit.

To change the colour of an individual entry in a data series:

❶ With the chart selected, click on an item (e.g. bar or line) in the data series – this will select the whole series.

❷ Double click on the individual entry that you wish to edit.

❸ Repeat steps 2–5 above.

Alternatively:

♦ Select a data series, e.g. a set of bars, and click the **Fill Color** drop down arrow on the Drawing toolbar. Experiment with the colours, or go into the **Fill Effects** dialog box to get the patterns and textures.

Formatting chart objects

You can format all types of chart objects, e.g. data series, chart title, gridlines, legend, axis:

❶ Double click on the object you wish to format.

❷ Select the options required from the **Formatting** dialog box.

❸ Click ⟨ OK ⟩.

Leaving the Graph environment

When your chart is complete, click anywhere on the slide outside the chart placeholder to return to your presentation. When you leave the Graph environment, the whole chart becomes an object within your presentation, and can be moved, copied, deleted or resized as necessary.

♦ If you wish to edit your chart, simply double click on it.

6.9 Organization charts

Organization charts give you another opportunity to make your point with a diagram rather than words. This section introduces Microsoft Organization Chart and some of its features. If you use a lot of organization charts, tour through its menus and the on-line Help to appreciate its full potential.

❶ Create a new slide with an organization chart placeholder on it.

❷   Double-click within the organization chart placeholder on your slide.

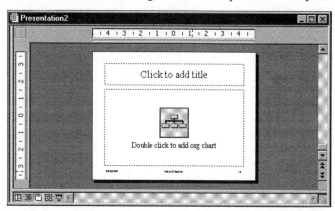

♦   Work out the structure you wish to display before you start.

Text and boxes

Organization charts can be very complicated structures but they have only simple elements. The small set of tools in this window is all that you need. Most are for adding boxes, and all the normal range of relationships are covered here.

To enter your text into a box:

❶   Click in the box you wish to edit.

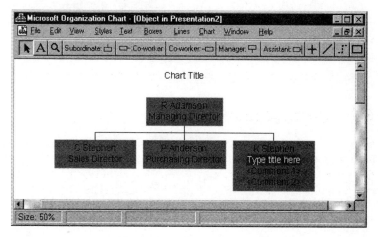

❷   Key in your data and press [Enter] or the arrow keys to move to the next row.

❸   Click on the next box to be completed, or anywhere outside the box, when you are finished.

Adding and deleting boxes

You can easily build your chart up by adding boxes where needed. Deleting boxes is even easier.

To add a box:

❶   Select the box type from the Toolbar.

❷   Click on the box to which the new box is related.

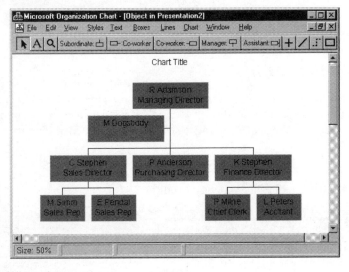

To delete a box:

❶   Click on it to select it, and press [Delete].

♦   If you change your mind, use Edit - Undo Delete to bring it back again.

Text and drawing tools

The text and drawing tools can be used to add the finishing touches to your organization chart. If you need text outside the boxes on your chart, use the **Text** tool.

Adding text:

❶ Click the **Text** tool .

❷ Click to position the insertion point.

❸ Key in the text.

❹ Click anywhere outside the text area to deselect the text and tool.

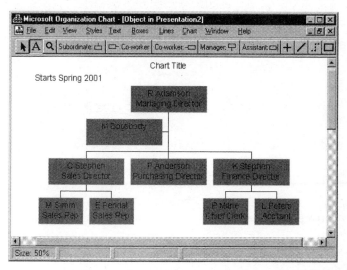

There are four drawing tools – three types of line and a box. These can be used to add extra lines or boxes (that are not part of the chart structure).

❶ Select a tool.

❷ Click and drag to draw the line or box.

♦ [Ctrl]-[D] toggles the display of the drawing tools on the toolbar.

Chart title

You can give your chart a title here or in the Slide Title area, in your presentation. If you opt for a title in the presentation, delete the Chart Title prompt.

❶ Select the **Chart Title** prompt.

❷ Key in the title.

Or

♦ Press [Delete] to remove the prompt.

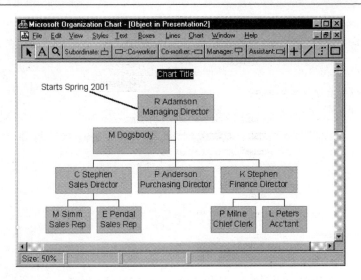

Zoom options

You can zoom in and out on the organization chart to get a closer look at what's there, or to get an overview of the whole thing. There are four options:

- ◆ Size to Window – for an overview of the whole chart.
- ◆ 50% of Actual – the best mode for normal work.
- ◆ Actual Size (100%) – in this mode the **Zoom** tool toggles to Size to Window.
- ◆ 200% of Actual – if you want to get really close.

To Zoom to Actual size:

❶ Select the **Zoom** tool 🔍 .

❷ Click where you want to zoom in on.

To Zoom out:

❶ Select the **Size to Window** tool 🔠 .

❷ Click on the chart – it reduces so you can see the entire chart in your window.

To return to Normal view

● Open the **View** Menu.

● Select **50% of Actual**.

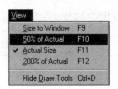

Finishing touches

Using the Boxes, Lines and Text menus, you can add the finishing touches to your organization chart – edit the line styles, add shadows to the boxes, change the colour, size and font of text, etc.

To restyle a box:

● Select the box(es).

● Open the **Boxes** menu and choose **Border**, **Shadow** or **Color**.

● Select an option.

To edit lines:

● Select the line(s).

● From the **Lines** menu choose **Thickness**, **Style** or **Color**.

● Select an option.

◆ To select several boxes or lines at once, select one then hold [Shift], and click on the others.

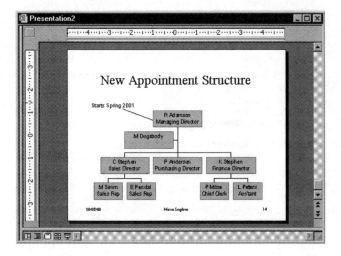

Update and exit

Once you've completed your organization chart, you will need to update the slide in your presentation and return to the presentation proper to continue working on it.

❶ Open the **File** menu.

❷ Choose **Update** *PRESENTATION NAME*.

◆ Your slide will now display your chart, but you are still in Organization Chart.

❸ Click the **Close** button on the Microsoft Organization Chart window title bar.

◆ To take your chart back into Organization Chart for editing, simply double click on it.

6.10 Tables

If you are accustomed to creating tables using Word, you'll find it very easy to create tables on your slides. The Tables are inserted as an object.

◆ Create a new slide with a Table placeholder set up.

❶ Double click on the Table placeholder on your slide.

❷ Specify the number of rows and columns you need.

❸ Click OK.

❹ Complete your table as required.

The Tables and Borders toolbar will appear when a table is selected. Use the tools on it to help you format your table attractively.

◆ If the toolbar doesn't appear, click the **Tables and Borders** tool on the Standard toolbar to display it.

When working in a table

- ◆ Press [Tab] to move to the next cell.

- ◆ Press [Shift]-[Tab] to go to the previous cell.

Or

- ◆ Use the arrow keys to move up, down, right and left.

Or

- ◆ Click in the cell you wish to work on.

- ◆ Click outside the table when you've finished.

- ◆ Click on your table again if you wish to edit it.

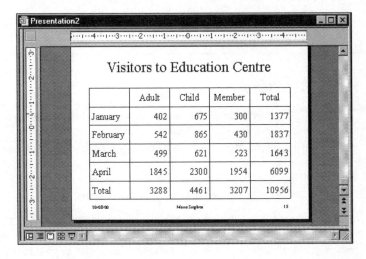

6.11 The Clip Gallery

PowerPoint comes with hundreds of clip art pictures that can be added to your slides. In addition to the clips that come with PowerPoint 2000, you'll find that you can access many more on the Internet.

- ◆ Set up a New Slide with a Clip Art placeholder on it.

- ❶ Double click within the Clip Art placeholder.

See 8.13 for more information on inserting clip art.

NOTES

You can easily add notes to your slides at any time. The notes are for the presenter's reference during the presentation.

To enter notes:

❶   Display the slide you want to prepare notes for in Normal view.

Or

❷   Select the slide in Outline View.

❸   Click in the notes pane.

❹   Type up the notes required.

The notes can be printed out – see section 6.15 below.

6.12   Masters

The slides, notes pages and handouts in a presentation all have a *master* or pattern on which they are based. If you want to change something, e.g. the font used or logo that appears on each slide, or switch headers or footers on or off, you can do so by editing the master (rather than the individual slide or notes page). Any changes made to a master will be reflected in every slide, notes page or handout based on that master.

There are two masters for your slides – the *title* slide master and the *slide* master. Changes to the title slide master will affect the title slide only; changes to the slide master will affect all the other slides in your presentation.

Slide Master

The Slide Master holds the formatted placeholders for the slide title and text. Changes to the Slide Master will be reflected in every slide in your presentation (except the Title Slide). Any slides where you have made changes to the text formatting at slide level will be treated as exceptions and will retain the custom formatting you applied to them.

Any background objects you want to appear on every slide (like your company name or logo) should be added to the Slide Master.

❶ Choose **Master** from the **View** menu.

❷ Select **Slide Master**.

❸ Amend the Slide Master as required (using the same techniques you use on a slide in your presentation).

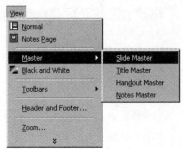

❹ Choose an alternative view to leave your Slide Master.

♦ If you hold down [Shift] and click the Slide View button , this takes you to the Slide Master, or to the Title Master if you are on the title slide at the time.

♦ The title slide has its own master. Changes made to the Slide Master will not be reflected on your Title slide.

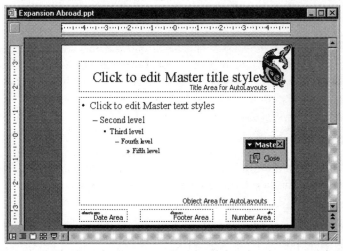

Title Master

You can view and edit the Title Master if you wish. Changes made to the Title Master will only affect the title slide, not the others in the presentation.

❶ Choose **Master** from the **View** menu.

❷ Select **Title Master**.

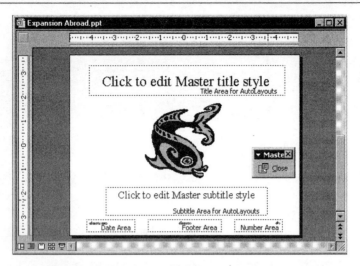

❸ Amend the Title Master as required (using the normal techniques).

❹ Choose an alternative view to leave your Title Master.

If you have no title master in your presentation you can add one (if you have used the Blank Presentation option you'll have no title master):

❶ View the **Slide Master**.

❷ Open the **Insert** menu.

❸ Choose **New Title Master**.

Handout/Notes Master

You can also edit the Handout or Notes master if required:

❶ Choose **Master** from the **View** menu.

❷ Select **Handout Master** or **Notes Master**.

❸ Edit the master as required.

❹ Choose an alternative view to leave your master.

The placeholders

The Date, Page Number, Header or Footer placeholders that are on all masters are optional. They can easily be deleted – or put back again if you decide you want them after all.

Deleting placeholders:

◆   Select the placeholder and press [Delete].

Restoring placeholders:

❶   Select **Master Layout...** (the option de-
    pends on what master you are looking
    at) from the Common Tasks list in your
    master layout view.

❷   Select the placeholders required.

❸   Click   OK   .

6.13   Slide Shows

Slide Sorter view

There are several useful features worth exploring in Slide Sorter view,
including:

◆   Hiding slides   ◆   Setting up transitions

◆   Animating text on slides   ◆   Rehearsing timings

Click the **Slide Sorter View** tool [⊞].

Slide Sorter toolbar

Slide Transition Effects, Preset Animation and Hide Slides can be specified in any view using the **Tools** menu, but I find it easiest to do them from
Slide Sorter view using the Slide Sorter toolbar.

Hide Slide

This option can prove useful if you're unsure whether or not you will really
need a particular slide for your presentation. You can include the slide in
your presentation (in case it's needed), but hide it. The hidden slide will
be by-passed during your slide show, unless you decide you need to use it.

❶   Select the slide you want to hide.

❷   Click the **Hide Slide** tool [▨].

◆   The number is crossed out under the slide.

- ◆ If you want to show the hidden slide during a presentation press [H] at the slide preceding the hidden one.

- ◆ To remove the hidden status from a slide, select it and click the **Hide Slide** tool again.

Transitions

A transition is an effect used between slides in a show. The default option is that No Transition is set, but there are several interesting alternatives that you might find effective for your presentation. The transition effect occurs as the slide that has the effect applied to it *appears* in your presentation.

❶ Select the slide that you wish to give a transition effect.

❷ Click the **Slide Transition** tool .

❸ Select the **Effect** from the drop down list.

❹ The Preview window demonstrates the effect – click on it to see the effect again.

❺ Set the Speed to Fast. Focus your audience on your slides, not the transition method!

❻ Choose an **Advance** option.

❼ Add a sound if wanted.

❽ Click **Apply** or **Apply to All** if you want the effect added to all your slides.

- ◆ If a transition is set, a transition icon appears below the slide in Slide Sorter view. Click on it to see the transition effect. You can also preview a transition by selecting the slide, then clicking the **Animation Preview** tool 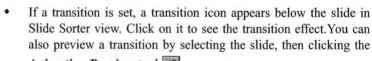.

- ◆ Use the Slide Show together with Slide Sorter view when experimenting with animation effects. Then you can check that the options you choose are having the desired effect.

Preset animations

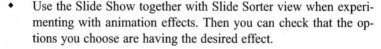

If you have several points listed in the body text of your slide, you could try building the slide up during the presentation, rather than presenting the whole list at once. Experiment with the Preset Animation options and effects until you find the ones you prefer. You can have a lot of fun messing about with the options available – but try to avoid having a different effect on each slide!

❶   Select the slide you wish to animate.

❷   Drop down the **Preset Animation** list on the Slide Sorter toolbar.

❸   Choose an effect.

◆   With your slide selected in Slide Sorter view, click the Slide Show icon, work through your slide then press [Esc] to return to Slide Sorter view.

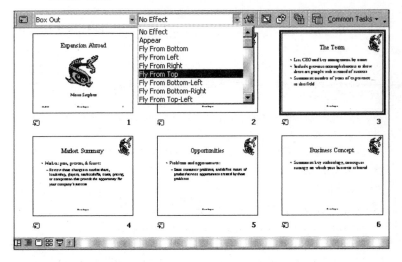

Rehearse timings

It is a very good idea to practise your presentation before you go in front of your audience. As well as practising what you intend to say (probably with the aid of notes you have made using the Notes Pages feature), you can rehearse the timings for each slide.

Click the **Rehearse Timings** tool 🕑 to take the slide show for a practice run!

❶   Go over what you intend to say while the slide is displayed.

❷   Click the left mouse button to move to the next slide when ready.

❸   Repeat steps 1 and 2 until you reach the end of your presentation.

A dialog box displays the total length of time your presentation took and asks if you want to record and use the new slide timings in a slide show. Choose **Yes**, if you want each slide to advance after the allocated time.

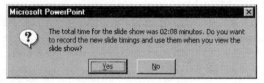

The slide timings will be displayed in Slide Sorter view.

◆   You can rehearse your timings as often as is necessary, until you've got the pace right to get your message across.

Summary Slide

You can get PowerPoint to automatically produce a Summary Slide for your presentation. The Summary Slide is placed in front of the other slides in your presentation. PowerPoint takes the title of each slide you select and lists it on the Summary Slide.

❶   Select the slides from which you wish to produce a Summary Slide.

❷   Click the **Summary Slide** tool 🗐 on the Slide Sorter toolbar.

◆   PowerPoint will generate as many Summary Slides as is necessary to list the title detail from all the slides you select.

6.14   Slide Show

You can run your slide show at any time to check how your presentation is progressing. Each slide fills the whole of your computer screen. After the last, you are returned to the view you were in when you clicked the **Slide Show** tool.

❶   Select the slide you want to start from, usually the first.

❷   Click the **Slide Show** icon 🖳 to the left of the horizontal scroll bar.

❸ Press [Page Down] or [Enter] (or click the left mouse button) to move onto the next slide.

◆ Press [Page Up] to move back to the previous slide if necessary.

◆ You can exit your slide show at any time by pressing the [Esc] key.

Working within your slide show

When presenting a slide show, you may want to leave the normal sequence, go directly to a slide, or draw on a slide to focus attention. These, and other features, can be accessed using the pop-up menu or the keyboard.

❶ Click the right mouse button or the pop-up menu icon at the bottom left corner of the screen.

To go directly to a slide:

❷ Select **Go**, then **By Title**.

❸ Choose the slide you want to go to.

◆ Experiment with the pop-up menu to see what options are available.

To 'draw' on your screen:

❶ Press **[Ctrl]-[P]** to change the mouse pointer to a pen.

❷ Click and drag to draw.

❸ Press **[Ctrl]-[A]** to change the pointer back to an arrow.

To erase your drawing:

❹ Press [E] on your keyboard.

◆ For more help on the options available to you while running Slide Show, press [F1] to open the **Slide Show Help** dialog box.

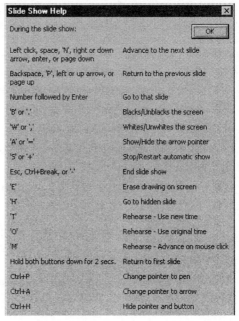

Slide Show Help	☒
During the slide show:	OK
Left click, space, 'N', right or down arrow, enter, or page down	Advance to the next slide
Backspace, 'P', left or up arrow, or page up	Return to the previous slide
Number followed by Enter	Go to that slide
'B' or '.'	Blacks/Unblacks the screen
'W' or ','	Whites/Unwhites the screen
'A' or '='	Show/Hide the arrow pointer
'S' or '+'	Stop/Restart automatic show
Esc, Ctrl+Break, or '-'	End slide show
'E'	Erase drawing on screen
'H'	Go to hidden slide
'T'	Rehearse - Use new time
'O'	Rehearse - Use original time
'M'	Rehearse - Advance on mouse click
Hold both buttons down for 2 secs.	Return to first slide
Ctrl+P	Change pointer to pen
Ctrl+A	Change pointer to arrow
Ctrl+H	Hide pointer and button

6.15 Printing presentations

You can print your whole presentation in PowerPoint – the slides, speaker's notes pages, audience handouts and the presentation outline.

The first stage to printing your presentation is to set up the format.

❶ Choose **Page Setup** from the **File** menu.

❷ Select the size from the **Slides sized for** field.

❸ Specify the orientation required for the **Slides**.

❹ Specify the orientation required for the **Notes, handouts & outline**.

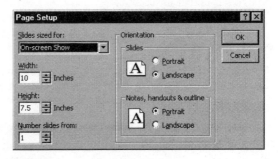

❺ Click **OK**.

♦ If you change the slide orientation, you may find that you need to change the size and shape of placeholders on the Slide Master to get your objects to fit well.

Printing

With the Page Setup details specified to give the output required, you can go ahead and print.

❶ Open the **File** menu and choose **Print**.

❷ Specify the **Print range** to print.

❸ Select the option required in the **Print what**: list.

Slides – prints the slides on paper or overhead transparencies, one per page.

Handouts – prints miniatures of the slides two, three, four, six or nine to the page. Printing your handouts with three slides to the page is particularly useful as there is room for your audience to make their own notes.

Notes Pages – prints a slide miniature, together with any notes that you have made to prompt you during your presentation.

Outline View – prints the text of each slide, showing the structure of the presentation.

❹   Click ▭ OK ▭.

◆   If you click the print icon on the Standard toolbar, one copy of each slide is printed. To print anything else you must access the **Print** dialog box and specify what you want in the **Print what:** field.

6.16   Mock test

Read the notes on *The tests* in the Preface. This test is in two parts. The first part tests your skills at setting up a new presentation, the second part sets you several tasks so that you can demonstrate your editing skills.

Preparation

Create a presentation and enter the four slides below. Save the presentation as *Mock Test*. Type in the text exactly as it appears in the slides below. Save and close the presentation file, and exit PowerPoint.

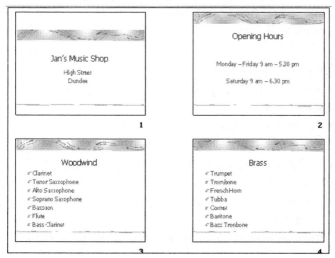

Remember that your real test will be closed book, so no cheating! Time yourself carefully – you should be able to complete the whole test within 45 minutes.

Test Part 1

The first task is to create a three-slide presentation for Capital Sports Ltd. **(15 marks)**

1. Open the presentation application.

2. The first slide is to be a Title slide; select the correct format for this slide.

3. Put the company name in the Title placeholder on the title slide: *Capital Sports Ltd.*

4. Create a business logo. You can draw it or find a suitable piece of ClipArt.

5. Insert the logo on the slide master (position it either top right or top left, whatever you think looks best) – so that it appears on all three slides without you having to add it to each one.

6. On the second slide create an organization chart for the company. It should have one person at the top and three people reporting. Create this diagram either by means of boxes which you draw yourself or by using facilities available in your presentation software.

7. Put a title on this slide: *Company Structure.*

8. Use bullets on Slide 3.

9. Put a title on this slide: *Senior Management – Capital Sports Ltd.*

10. Introduce the senior management on slide three as follows:
    Pam Simpson – Managing Director
    Robert Peters – Finance
    Gill Adams – Marketing
    James Burns – Purchasing

11. Format each person's name bold.

12. Change the font colour for *Capital Sports Ltd* on Slide 3.

13. Change the organization chart on Slide 2 to include the names and positions of senior management (see 10 above)

14. Print handouts for the presentation, three slides to a page.

15. Close the presentation, saving the presentation as *Capital Sports* on your disk.

Test Part 2

The second task is to change the *Mock Test* presentation (the one shown in *Preparation* above). **(15 marks)**

1. Open the presentation called *Mock Test*.

2. Delete Slide 2.

3. Change the layout of the new Slide 2 to include a ClipArt placeholder (as well as the bulleted list).

4. Insert an appropriate piece of ClipArt into the new Slide 2.

5. Apply a different design template to the presentation.

6. Change the layout of Slide 3 (Brass) to one with two sets of bulleted lists.

7. Add '*& Percussion*' to the slide title.

8. Type the following list of percussion instruments on the right of Slide 3:

   ◆ Keyboards

   ◆ Snare Drum

   ◆ Timpani

   ◆ Vibraphone

   ◆ Xylophone

   ◆ Side Drum

   ◆ Bass Drum

9. Number the slides.

10. Spell check the presentation and make changes where necessary.

11. Print handouts for the presentation, two slides to a page.

12. Change the orientation to landscape and print the handouts for the presentation again, three slides to a page.

13. Add some speaker's notes that you might use in your presentation to Slide 2 (Woodwind).

14. Save the file as *Mock Test Edit*.

15. Close the application.

SUMMARY

In this chapter you found out how to create presention files. We have discussed:

✓ The content of a presentation file – slides, handouts, notes, outline.

✓ Adding slides to the presentation.

✓ Slide layout.

✓ Design Templates.

✓ The structure of bullet points.

✓ Charts on slides.

✓ Tables on slides.

✓ Organization charts on slides.

✓ Hide slide, transitions, animations, rehearse timings and summary slide.

✓ Giving a presentation.

✓ Printing the presentation file.

7 | INFORMATION AND COMMUNICATION

AIMS OF THIS CHAPTER

This chapter discusses the Internet and e-mail. The browser used is Internet Explorer from Microsoft, and the e-mail application is Outlook Express. These are probably the most widely used browser and e-mail applications. The topics discussed in this chapter will help prepare you for the Module 7 ECDL test.

7.1 First steps with the Internet

To open your browser application:

* Double click the Internet Explorer shortcut on your desktop.

Or

* On the **Start** menu, choose **Programs**, and click **Internet Explorer**.

If you have a dial-up connection (one where you connect to your Internet Service Provider (ISP), and through them to the Internet over the public telephone lines, you'll be asked for your user name and password.

* Complete the dialog box.

The page that appears on your screen when you open your browser application is your *Home Page*.

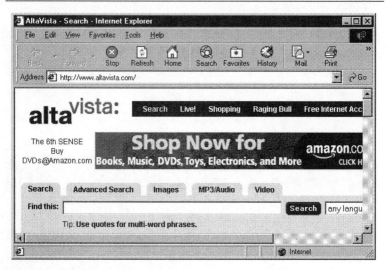

You can visit any page on the Web by entering the URL in the Address field. A web page is a screen display that may contain text, graphics, sound, etc. If the information you want to make available on the Web would be better set up on several pages, you can set up a number of pages and link them together. Most organizations do this to set up a web *site*.

URL (Uniform Resource Locator)

The URL is the address of the page you wish to visit.

What do the URLs mean?

http:// identifies the address as a WWW (World Wide Web) URL.

www is how WWW addresses usually start (but not always, e.g. **http://news.bbc.co.uk/**)

Some URLs are very short, e.g. **http://www.coke.com/**

This address takes you to the Coke website, a commercial organization in the USA.

Others are more complex, e.g. **http://www.orknet.co.uk/lows/index.htm**

This one takes you to the home page (**index.htm**) of a company called **Lows**. The site has been set up by a UK company – **orknet.co.uk** gives us this information.

You will find Web addresses *everywhere*. In newspapers and magazines, on the TV, on items that you buy, etc. Make a note of any that sound interesting so that you can give them a visit.

♦   If you know the URL of a web page that you wish to visit, simply key it into the Address field and press [Enter].

Home Page

The Home Page is the one that is displayed when you open your browser application. It is also the one that you are returned to when you click HOME on the toolbar.

You can easily change your Home Page if you wish – you might want your favourite search engine to be your Home Page, or your own web page.

To change the Home Page:

❶   Locate the page you wish to use for your Home Page.

❷   Open the **Tools** menu and choose **Internet Options...**

❸   Select the **General** tab.

❹   Click **Use Current**.

❺   Click **OK**.

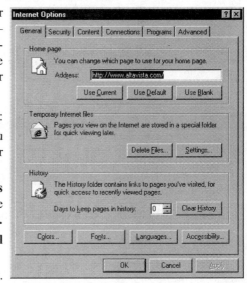

Saving a Web page

If you find a page that you want to be able to view or print later when you are not connected to the Internet, you should save it.

❶   Open the **File** menu.

❷   Choose **Save As...**

❸   Specify the drive/folder that you want the page on.

❹   Accept or edit the file name.

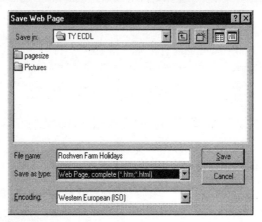

⑤ Specify the **Save as** type option required.

⑥ Click **Save**.

Help

The Help system is very similar to Windows help and those in other applications. The Help menu gives you access to the various help areas.

Try the Tour – you'll find lots of useful information and tips to help get you started.

You'll find more information on Help in Chapters 2 and 8.

Ending an online session

❶ Close the Web browsing application.

❷ Click the **Close** button at the right of the title bar and disconnect from your ISP (unless you are connected to a LAN).

7.2 Internet settings

View/Display modes

You can customize the way that your browser window looks by selecting from the various view options.

You can elect to display various Explorer bars to help you with your work.

The Explorer bars are Favorites, Search and History.

To display an Explorer bar:

◆ Click a tool to toggle its display in the Explorer bar.

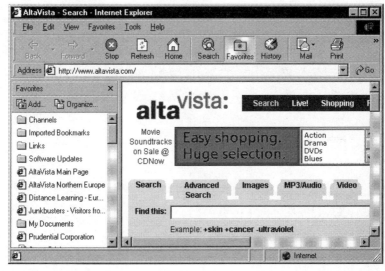

Toolbar display

The toolbars that are normally displayed are the Standard buttons and the Address bar. There are a couple of others – Links and Radio – that you can display if you wish.

To switch a toolbar on or off:

❶ Open the **View** menu.

❷ Choose **Toolbars**.

❸ Select or deselect the toolbar as required.

◆ To the left of each toolbar you will see a raised 'handle'. You can move your toolbars by dragging these handles if necessary.

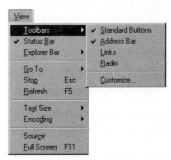

Customizing toolbars

You can customize the Standard toolbar if you wish.

❶   Open the **View** menu, choose Toolbars then click **Customize...**

Or

◆   Right click on a toolbar, then choose **Toolbars** and click **Customize...** on the shortcut menu.

❷   **Add** or **Remove** tools from the lists as required.

❸   Close the dialog box when you've finished.

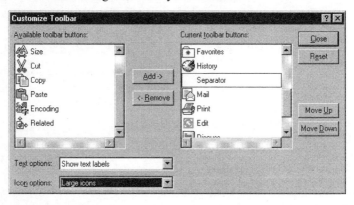

Display/hide images

Most Web pages have pictures on them. Some pages are slow to download because of the pictures – the files are so big it takes time to transfer them to your PC. To help speed up the display of your Web pages, you can turn the graphics off.

To switch off graphics:

❶   Open the **Tools** menu and choose **Internet Options...**

❷   Click the **Advanced** tab.

❸   In the **Multimedia** area, deselect the **Show pictures** option (and/ or **Play animations**, **Play videos**, or **Play sounds** as required).

◆   You can still display an individual picture or animation on a Web page even if you have deselected the **Show pictures** or **Play videos** options. Right click on its icon and then click **Show Picture**.

♦   If the pictures on the current page are still visible after you clear
    the Show pictures check box, open the **View** menu and click **Re-
    fresh** to hide them.

♦   If you wish to set up your system to display pictures again, repeat
    steps 1-3, selecting the checkboxes required.

♦   If a page is downloading too slowly, you can click 🔲 to stop it.

♦   If a page isn't displaying correctly (or if it might have been updated

    since you displayed it) you can refresh it by clicking 🔲.

7.3   Web navigation

If you know the URL of the web page or site you can easily go to it.

❶   Enter its URL in the **Address** field.

❷   Press [Enter].

Hyperlink

Many of the pages that you visit will have hyperlinks to other pages or
sites that you may be interested in. A hyperlink is a 'hot spot' that lets you
jump from one place on a page to another or from one page to another, or
to a different site altogether.

Hyperlinks

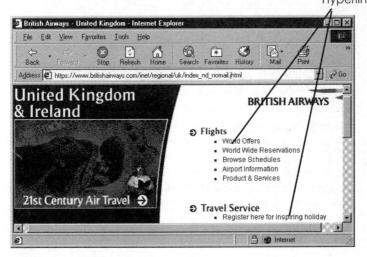

Many hyperlinks are text – usually coloured blue with a blue underline.

Hyperlinks may also be a picture – if you position the mouse pointer over a picture hyperlink it becomes a hand with a pointing finger.

♦   To jump to the location that the hyperlink points to, just click on it.

As you jump from one location to another following the hyperlinks that interest you, you are *surfing* the net.

As you surf, you may want to revisit pages or sites you have already been to. You could:

♦   Click the ⟵ Back and ⟶ Forward tools on the Standard toolbar to move between the pages you've already visited.

Or

♦   Click History and select the URL of the page you wish to return to.

7.4   Web searching

If you don't know the URL of the page or site you want you will need to search for it. If you are looking for information on a topic you would search for the information required. The result of a search is a list of several (sometimes thousands) of pages or sites you may be interested in.

You could perform a limited search using Explorer's Search facility.

❶   Click **Search** on the Standard toolbar to display the Search panel.

❷   Chose the category, **Find a Web page**.

❸   Enter the word or words you are searching for – the more information you give, the more appropriate the results will be. For example, if you are looking for restaurants in Edinburgh, but not Chinese ones, enter **+Edinburgh +Restaurant -Chinese** in the search field (+ means that the page must contain that word, - means that the page must not).

❹   Click **Search**.

The Search panel will display a list of matching sites. Scroll through the list to see what's there. If you can't see anything that interests you, click **Next** at the bottom of the list to display more sites.

If you find a site listed that you want to visit, click on it. The site will be displayed on your screen.

If you want to perform a new search, click the **New** tool at the top of the panel and try again.

Close the Search panel when you've found your page so that you can see it better.

Experiment with the Search panel.

Search engines

You can also search using a search engine. There are many of these, including AltaVista (http://www.altavista.com), Yahoo (http://www.yahoo.com), Lycos (http://www.lycos.com) and Excite (http://www.excite.com). The one used in this example is AltaVista.

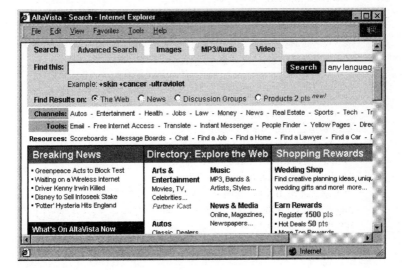

Most search engines have a 'directory' to allow you to locate the information you require by working through the various topics. However, if you know what you're looking for it's usually quicker to *search*. In AltaVista you can specify the keywords and phrases in the **Find this:** field.

In this example the search is for short breaks in Speyside. Sites that have details of camping are not required, but I want sites that mention skiing.

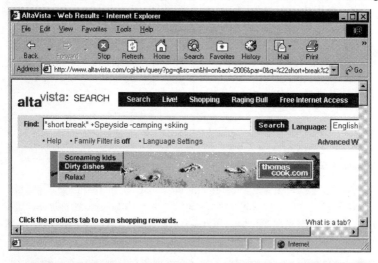

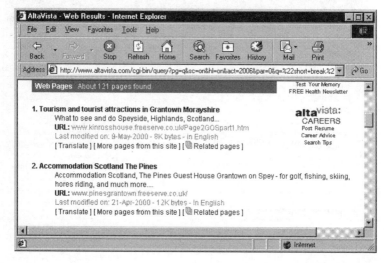

You will notice that:

* Phrases are enclosed within double quotes, e.g. "short breaks".

* Words that should be included are preceded by a plus, e.g. +Speyside.

* To exclude a word, precede it by a minus, e.g. -camping.

Look through the list of sites found – you may find you have hundreds of thousands of them (if this is the case you need to be much more precise in stating your search requirements). My search turned up 121 pages.

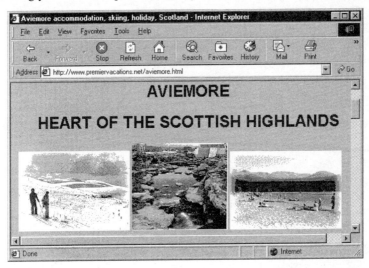

7.4   Favorites

If you find a site that you know you will want to revisit, you should add it to your list of Favorites. You can then access the site easily without having to enter the URL or search it out.

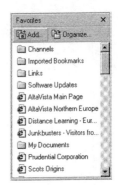

❶ Display the page that you want to add to your list of Favorites.

❷ Click [Favorites] on the Standard toolbar to display the Favorites panel.

❸ Click **Add** at the top of the panel.

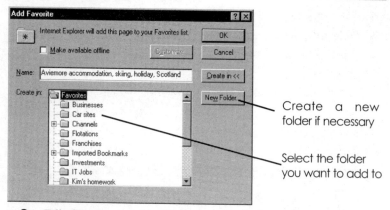

Create a new folder if necessary

Select the folder you want to add to

❹ Edit the page name in the **Name** field if you wish.

❺ Select the folder that you want to add your page to.

❻ Click **OK**.

To go to a page in your favourites list:

❶ Display the **Favourites** panel.

❷ Open the folder that contains your favourite.

❸ Click on the page required.

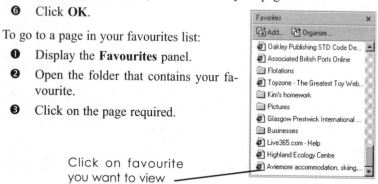

Click on favourite you want to view

As you use the Internet your list of Favorites will most probably get larger. If necessary you can set up folders to help you organize your Favorites and move or delete Favorites as necessary.

To create a new folder:

❶ Go into **Organize Favorites** – click **Organize...** at the top of the Favorites panel.

❷ Click **Create Folder**.

❸ Give your folder a name.

To Rename an item:

❶ Select it.

❷ Click **Rename**.

❸ Type in a new name.

❹ Press [Enter].

To move an item:

❶ Select it.

❷ Click **Move to Folder...**

❸ Select the folder you wish to move it to.

❹ Click **OK**.

The favourite's properties

To delete an item:

❶ Select it.

❷ Click **Delete**.

❸ Click **Yes** to confirm the deletion.

To view the properties of a favourite, or to make it available offline:

❶ Select the favourite.

❷ Read the properties.

❸ Select or deselect the **Make available offline** option as required.

❹ **Close** the **Organize Favorites** dialog box when you've finished.

7.5 Collecting information

If you find a web page that contains information that would be useful for a report, paper or essay that you are working on you can easily collect the information into a Word document. As you work you may collect information from many different sources and add them to your document.

To collect information:

❶ Select the text that you require from a web page.

❷ Open the **Edit** menu and choose **Copy**.

❸　Go to or open Word.

❹　Create a new document (or open an existing document) to paste your text into.

❺　Position the insertion point where you want the text to appear.

❻　Click the **Paste** tool.

You can add more information to your document as you find it, edit the text, save the document and print it as required.

7.6　Printing

If you find a web page that you would like to print you can do so easily.

Page Setup

You might want to check/change the page setup options.

❶　Open the **File** menu.

❷　Choose **Page Setup**.

❸　Edit the fields as required, e.g. change orientation or page size.

❹　Click **OK**.

Print

❶　Click the **Print** tool on the Standard toolbar.

Or

❷　Open the **File** menu and choose **Print**.

❸　Set the Print options required.

❹　Click **OK**.

7.7　Starting to use e-mail

Opening your e-mail application

You can open your e-mail application through the Start menu in the same way as any other, e.g. Start, Programs, Outlook Express, or double click the Outlook Express shortcut on the desktop.

◆　Enter your username and password. Your Inbox will probably be displayed.

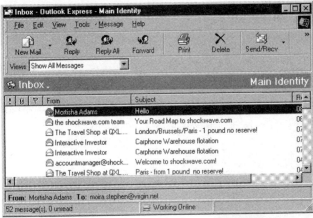

- If your Inbox isn't displayed, click the drop down arrow to the right of the area identifier – here showing **Inbox** – in the Folders bar and select **Inbox** from the list.

To read a message that is in your Inbox:

- Double click on a message to open it. If the preview pane is displayed, you can read the message in there rather than double click to open a separate window.

Help

The Help system is very similar to that found in Windows and in the other applications in the Office suite.

To access the on-line Help:

❶ Open the **Help** menu and choose **Contents and Index**.

Or

- Press **[F1]**.

❷ Use the **Contents**, **Index** or **Search** tabs to help you locate the information you require.

❸ **Close** the Help window when you've finished.

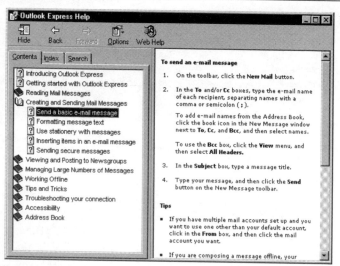

You'll find more information on working with Help in Chapters 2 and 8.

Display options

The appearance of your e-mail window may be different to the screenshots in this book. You can change the way that your screen looks by switching different areas on and off – it's really a matter of personal preference.

To change the appearance of your screen, open the **View** menu and choose **Layout...**

Experiment with the options in the **Layout** dialog box and see which setup appeals to you most.

You can customize the toolbar options from here too. Click **Customize Toolbar...** and add, remove or move the buttons as required.

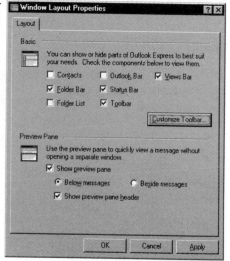

7.8   Create and send

♦ If necessary, open Outlook Express.

It is usually a good idea to work offline when composing your mail messages, especially if you're paying for your ISP connection (it helps keep your bills down!).

To work offline, disconnect from your ISP.

To create a new message and send it:

❶ Click [New Mail] to create a new mail message.

❷ Complete the **New Mail** dialog box (see notes below).

❸ Click [Send] when you've finished.

If you're working offline, the message will be placed in your Outbox when you click **Send**.

Messages placed in your Outbox will be sent when you click .

To: Cc: and Bcc:

Type the address of each recipient into the appropriate field (if there is more than one address, separate them with a semi colon ;).

♦ The **To:** field is for the main recipient(s).

♦ The **Cc:** field is for those that you want to send a copy so they know what's going on.

♦ The **Bcc:** field is for sending someone a *blind* copy. Only the message sender and the individual(s) in the **Bcc:** field know to whom the message has been sent. If the **Bcc:** field isn't displayed and you want to use it, open the **View** menu and choose **All Headers**.

Or

Add the addresses from the Address book (to open the address book, click the icon to the left of the **To** field)

❶ Select the name in the list.

❷ Click the **To: Cc:** or **Bcc:** buttons to specify the field that the address should be added to.

❸ Click **OK**.

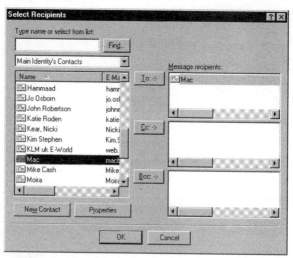

Subject field

Type the message title in the Subject field – this will be displayed in the inbox of the recipient, so they have an idea what the message is about.

Message area

Type your message in here. You can format the text using the formatting tools at the top of the message area if you wish.

Spell check

It's a good idea to spell-check messages before you send them. Click . See Chapter 8 for information on spell-checking if necessary.

Attach file

You might want to send an existing file to someone – a report or a workbook that you want them to see.

To attach a file:

❶ Click ⌷ Attach .

❷ Locate the file that you wish to attach – identify the drive and/or folder in the **Look In** field.

❸ Select the file.

❹ Click **Attach**.

◆ If you have more than one file to attach, repeat as necessary.

◆ If you attach a file by accident, select it in the Attach field and press [Delete].

Signature

If you end all your e-mail messages in the same way, you can automate this process by creating a *signature*. The signature can then be added to all e-mails automatically, or you can insert it when you wish.

To create a signature:

❶ In **Outlook Express** (*not* your new mail window), open the **Tools** menu and choose **Options**.

❷ Select the **Signatures** tab.

❸ Click **New**.

❹ Enter the text you want to show in the **Edit Signature** area.

❺ Select/deselect the **Add signatures to all outgoing messages**

checkbox as required.

❻ Click **OK**.

If you selected the **Add signatures to all outgoing messages** checkbox, all outgoing messages will automatically have the signature attached to them.

If you didn't opt to add the signature automatically, you can add it manually as required.

To add a signature to a message:

❶   Place the insertion point in the message area of your e-mail, where you want the signature to appear.

❷   Open the **Insert** menu.

❸   Choose **Signature**.

Priority

The priority option for messages is set to *Normal*. When messages have normal priority nothing appears in the priority field in the recipient's inbox. However, if you wish a message to be flagged as having a high priority ⵑ (to alert the recipient to the fact it is important that they read the message) or low priority ↓ (to let the recipient know they can leave it for the time being if they're busy!) you can do so.

To set the priority option to High or Low:

❶   Click the drop down arrow beside the **Priority** tool.

❷   Select the priority option required.

Cut/Copy/Paste

As you compose your message, you will probably need to edit it so that it says exactly what you want it to say. You can edit your text by inserting and deleting as necessary (just as you would in Word). You can also **Cut**, **Copy** and **Paste** if necessary to get your text where you want it. See Chapter 8 if you need information on how to use these tools.

You should be able to use the cut, copy and paste tools to move and copy text:

◆   from one place to another within a message.

◆   from one message to another message.

◆   from another source, e.g. Word into your e-mail message.

7.9   Receiving mail

We discussed opening and reading mail in *Starting to use e-mail* (7.7).

Reading an attachment

If a message has an attachment, a paperclip icon will be displayed beside it. If you have the preview pane displayed, a paperclip appears on the right of the preview pane header when the message is selected.

When you open the message, the name of the attachment will be displayed in the Attach field. The attachment name will have an icon beside it to indicate what application it was created in, e.g..

*   Double click on the attachment name to open it.

The attachment will be opened in the application required to display it, e.g. Word.

Save attachment

From an open message:

❶   Open the **File** menu.

❷   Choose **Save Attachments**

❸   Select the attachment(s).

❹   Locate the folder to save them in.

❺   Click **Save**.

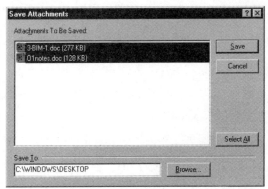

Or, if the message isn't open:

❶   Click the paperclip on the preview pane header.

❷   Choose **Save Attachments...**

❸   Follow steps 3-5 above.

*   You can also save an attachment from the application in which it is opened using **File**, **Save As...**

Reply

Messages that you receive may be read then:

*   replied to
*   have a reply sent to all on the original distribution list
*   forwarded to another address.

To reply, reply to all or forward a message:

❶   Select the message in your Inbox – click on it.

Or

◆   Open the message – double click on it.

❷   Click the **Reply, Reply to All** or **Forward** tool (depending on what you wish to do).

❸   If you are forwarding the message, enter the address in the **To: Cc:** and **Bcc:** fields as necessary.

❹   Complete the message (in same way as you would a new message).

❺   Click **Send**.

If you are replying to a message (using reply or reply to all) you may or may not want to include the original message in your reply. You can switch the include original message option on or off as required.

From your Inbox:

❶   Open the **Tools** menu.

❷   Choose **Options**.

❸   Select the **Send** tab.

❹   Under the Sending heading, select or deselect the *Include message in reply* checkbox as necessary

❺   Click **OK**.

You can then use Reply or Reply to All as above.

7.10   Address Book

Using the Address Book can save you a lot of time as you don't have to type the addresses into your messages each time you send one. To manage your Address Book efficiently you must be able to:

*   add addresses
*   delete addresses
*   update the address book from incoming mail
*   create a distribution list.

To add an address:

❶   Open the **Address Book** – click [Addresses] on the toolbar.

❷   In the Address Book, click **New**, then **New Contact...**

❸   Select the **Name** tab in the **Properties** dialog box.

❹   Enter the details.

❺   Click **OK**.

To delete an address:

❶   Open the **Address Book**.

❷   Scroll through the list of names until you see the one you want to delete.

❸   Select the name – click on it.

❹   Click the **Delete** tool or press [Delete].

❺   Respond to the prompt asking if you are sure that you want to delete.

To add an address to your Address Book from a message:

❶   Select the message in your Inbox.

❷   Open the **Tools** menu.

❸   Click **Add Sender to Address Book**.

Distribution lists

If you send e-mails to a group of people, e.g. others in your department or a group of committee members, you can set up a distribution list for the group. This can save time when it comes to addressing your e-mails to that group as all you need do is add the group name to the **To:** field and everyone in the group will receive the message.

❶   Open the **Address Book**.

❷   In the Address Book, click **New**, then **New Group...**

❸   On the **Group** tab, enter a name in the **Group Name** field.

◆   If details of a group member are already in the Address Book.

❹   Click **Select Members**.

❺   Select the members from your address list.

❻   Click **OK**.

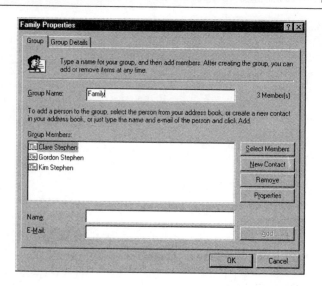

Or

+ If details of a group member are not in the **Address Book**:

❼ Click **New Contact** and add the details as above in *To add an address*.

Or

❽ Enter the name and e-mail of the person you want in the group and click **Add**.

❾ Click **OK** at the Properties dialog box when the group is complete.

Your group will be listed in your address book.

+ If you wish to edit the group, double click on it in the address book and add or remove members as necessary.

+ To send a message to a group, enter the group name into the **To:** field.

+ To delete a group, select it in the address book and press [Delete].

+ To send a reply to the sender and everyone in the group to which a message is sent use Reply to All.

7.11   Message management

As time goes by the number of e-mails you receive will increase. You will need to organize your messages so that you can keep track of them.

Find

If you have lost a message, you could try the **Find** command to help you locate it.

❶   Select the folder you wish to search – Inbox, Outbox, Sent Items, etc.

❷   Open the **Edit** menu.

❸   Click **Find**.

❹   Select **Message**.

❺   Enter the details you know into the **Find Message** dialog box (leave any fields you're not sure of blank).

❻   Click **Find Now**.

Mail folders

Create new mail folder:

❶   Open the **File** menu.

❷   Choose **Folder**.

❸   Click **New...**

❹   Enter a name for your folder.

❺   Select the folder that you wish to create your new folder within.

❻   Click **OK**.

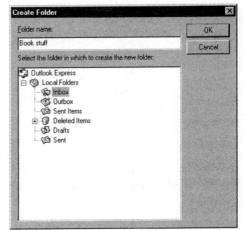

To move a message to a new mail folder:

❶   Select the message you wish to move.

❷   Open the **Edit** menu.

❸   Choose **Move to Folder...**

❹   Select the folder you wish to move the message to and click **OK**.

To view the contents of your new folder:

◆   Click the drop down arrow on the folder bar and select the folder
    required.

To delete message

❶   Select the message in your folder.

❷   Click **Delete** on the toolbar or press [Delete].

Sort messages by name, subject, date, etc

Your messages can be sorted into ascending or descending order. You can
sort on the *From* field, *Subject* or *Received* time of the message.

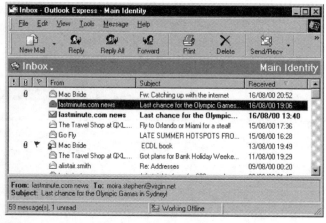

To change the sort order:

◆   Click the column heading at the top of the field you wish to sort,
    e.g. click on Subject to sort it in subject order.

A small triangle/arrow will appear on the column heading to indicate the
sort order – ascending or descending. Click the column heading again to
change the sort order.

Exiting Outlook Express

To close Outlook Express:

◆   Click the **Close** button at the right of the title bar.

7.12 Mock test

The following mock tests are similar to those you will find in the ECDL test. However, the site that you will visit then will have been set up specifically for the test – in the mock I've suggested a site anyone can visit.

♦   If the web site isn't available any site will do, just make sure that you can do everything that is asked of you in the mocks.

In the e-mail test, you will be given an e-mail account specifically for the test, and you will be asked to send and reply to e-mails from the ECDL tester. In the mocks I have suggested you use a friend instead – but you should perhaps warn them first!

You will be given an Answer File on disk, similar to the one below, into which you will be asked to type answers to some of the questions. You could create a file with this layout for a practice run if you wish.

Answer File

Name:	
1	
2	
3	
4	
5	
6	
7	
8	
9	
10	
11	
12	
13	
14	
15	

The test is divided into two sections, one testing your Internet skills, the other testing your e-mail skills. Both parts have equal weighting (15 marks), giving 30 marks for the whole test. You must score at least 24/30 to pass.

Test Part 1

1. Open a Web browsing application. **(1 mark)**

2. How do you change the Home Page in your web browsing application? Enter your answer under the appropriate question number in the Answer File. **(1 mark)**

3. Open the URL or web address: **http://www.holidaysafloat.co.uk** **(1 mark)**

4. Navigate from the *Welcome* page to the *Caley Cruisers* page using the hyperlink provided (you'll need to scroll down the page a bit). **(1 mark)**

5. Copy two lines of text from the *Caley Cruisers* page as your answer into the *Answer File* and save. **(1 mark)**

6. Open the hyperlink entitled *Barnes Brinkcraft* on the *Welcome* page. Browse the *Barnes Brinkcraft* page for information about prices. Copy two lines of information about prices and paste the information into the *Answer File*. Save the *Answer File*. **(1 mark)**

7. Describe how you would display and hide the *Favorites* bar. Enter your answer in the *Answer File* and save. **(1 mark)**

8. Use the application Help function to find information about *cookies*. Enter three lines of text information about *cookies* as your answer in the *Answer File* and save. **(1 mark)**

9. Access a search engine and enter the keyword *Camping* in a search. Enter a relevant hyperlink from the search results as your answer in the *Answer File* and save. **(1 mark)**

10. Refine your search to include *Camping* in *France*. Enter details of a relevant web address that has resulted from the search as your answer in the *Answer File* and save. **(1 mark)**

11. Print one page from the search report (list of sites found) on *Camping* in *France* as a printed document to a printer if available or as a print file on your disk if you haven't a printer available. **(1 mark)**

12. Go to URL **http://www.chantaco.com/bg.html** and use the hyperlink to go to the page *Facilites*. Print the page to a printer if available or as a print file on your disk. **(1 mark)**

13. Save the *Caley Cruisers* page as a file on your disk. **(1 mark)**

14. Describe how you would add the *Holidays Afloat* web page to your favourites folder. Enter your answer in the *Answer File* and save. **(1 mark)**

15. Close the Web browsing application. **(1 mark)**

Test Part 2

1. Open an electronic mail application and log on to your account. **(1 mark)**

2. Create an auto-signature for your e-mails. **(1 mark)**

3. Display the contents of your inbox. You are going to compose and send an e-mail message. Create a new mail message and enter the following short text:

   Jack,

   Please bring conference papers to meeting tomorrow

   Regards,

   Miriam **(1 mark)**

4. Insert a friend's e-mail address in the message *to* field, and the title *Conference meeting* in the message *subject* field. **(1 mark)**

5. Attach a file to the mail message. **(1 mark)**

6. Add an auto-signature to the message. **(1 mark)**

7. Send the message with a high priority. **(1 mark)**

8. Forward a message from your inbox to a friend. **(1 mark)**

9. Create another e-mail message with an addressee in the *to* field and a different addressee in the *cc* field. **(1 mark)**

10. Open any Word file on your disk (you will be given a file in the actual ECDL test) and copy some text from this file into the new message. **(1 mark)**

11. Copy text from any other e-mail and paste this text into your new message. Send the message. **(1 mark)**

12. Reply to a message from a friend with the original message included – add *No problem, thanks a lot* at the top of the message. **(1 mark)**

13. What are the benefits of using a distribution list in e-mail. Enter your answer in the *Answer File* and save. **(1 mark)**

14. Give a brief description of the *Reply to All* feature in e-mail. Enter your answer in the *Answer File* and save. **(1 mark)**

15. Close the electronic mail application. **(1 mark)**

SUMMARY

In this chapter you have learnt how to:

✓ Access the Internet.

✓ Locate a web site or page using a URL.

✓ Specify your Home Page.

✓ Save a web page to disk.

✓ Use the Help system.

✓ Change your toolbar display.

✓ Display/hide images on a web page.

✓ Use Hyperlinks to jump from one page to another.

✓ Search the web for sites that may be of interest to you.

✓ Add a URL to your Favourites folder.

✓ Copy information from a web page into a file.

✓ Print a web page.

✓ Read a message in your Inbox.

✓ Create, send and reply to e-mail messages.

✓ Access the Help system.

✓ Change your display settings.

✓ Add details to the *To*, *Cc* and *Bcc* fields.

✓ Add a signature to your message.

✓ Specify the message priority.

✓ Cut/copy and paste text from one message to another or from a different file into your e-mail message.

✓ Read an attachment.

✓ Attach a file to an e-mail message.

✓ Add, delete and edit Contacts in Address book.

✓ Manage your messages.

8 | COMMON SKILLS

AIMS OF THIS CHAPTER

The applications (Word, Excel, PowerPoint, Access) discussed in this book are all part of the Microsoft Office suite. As the packages belong to the same suite, many commands and routines, e.g. save, copy, and spell-check are the same (or very similar) in each application. This chapter discusses these features. You should read through this chapter *before* going onto the chapters discussing the individual applications, and refer back to it as necessary.

8.1   Opening and closing an application

The Start menu

❶   Click the **Start** button on the Taskbar.

❷   Choose **Programs**.

❸   Click the application, e.g. Microsoft Excel; Accessories, WordPad; Accessories, Games, Solitaire, etc.

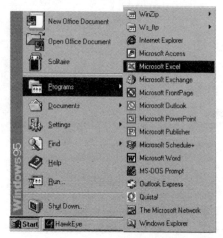

The Shortcut Bar

As an alternative to using the **Start** menu on the Taskbar, you could use the Shortcut Bar.

If the application tool is on the Shortcut Bar, e.g. Excel ![icon], just click it!

Closing an application

Click the **Close** button ![x] at the right of the application Title Bar.

8.2 Application window

You should be able to recognize the following areas in the application windows:

- Toolbars, e.g. Standard, Formatting
- Menu Bar
- Minimize button
- Title Bar
- Status Bar
- Close button
- Window Border
- Maximize/Restore button

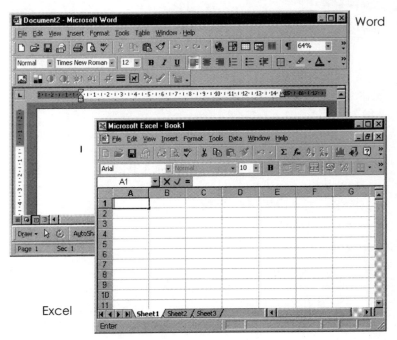

Word

Excel

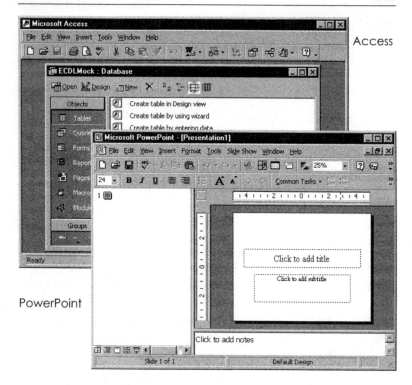

Access

PowerPoint

8.3 File handling

Save and Save As

If you want to keep your file, you must save it. If you don't save your file, the data will be lost when you exit your application. You can save your file at any time – you don't have to wait until you've entered all your text or data and corrected all the errors.

To save your file:

❶ Click the **Save** tool 🔳 on the Standard toolbar.

❷ At the **Save As** dialog box select the folder you want to save your file into (the default is the Desktop in WordPad, My Documents in Office applications).

❸   Give your file a name.

❹   Leave the **Save as type:** at the default, e.g. Word Document in Word, Microsoft Excel Workbook in Excel, Word for Windows 6.0 in WordPad.

❺   Click **Save**.

✦   The name of your file will appear on the Title Bar in place of the temporary file name.

As your document develops, you can re-save your file any time you wish – just click the **Save** tool again. The **Save As** dialog will not re-appear, but the old version of the file on your disk will be replaced by the new, up-to-date version displayed on your screen.

Save As

There may be times that you save a file, edit it, then decide that you want to save the edited file but also keep the original version of the file on disk.

If you don't want to overwrite the old file with the new version, you should save it using a different file name or to a different drive and/or folder.

❶   Open the **File** menu and choose **Save As**.

❷   The **Save As** dialog box will appear again.

❸   Change the drive or folder if you wish.

❹   Enter a new name in the *File name* field.

❺   Click **Save**.

Exchanging files

There may be times when you create a file in one application, and then need to save it in a different file format because the file is going to be opened in another application, e.g. Write, Works, WordPad, an earlier version of Word or on a web site.

In these situations you must save your file in a file format that can be opened by the destination application.

To save in a different file format:

❶   Click the **Save** tool or choose **Save As** from the file menu if you've already saved the file.

❷   Select the drive and/or folder and name the file as usual.

❸   Select the appropriate file format from the **Save as type:** options.

❹   Click **Save**.

Close file

Once you've finished working on your file you should close it.

To close your file:

◆   Open the **File** menu and choose **Close**.

Or

◆   Click the **Close** button ⊠ at the top right of the file title bar.

You will be prompted to save the file if it has changed since the last time you saved it.

Create a new file

It is very easy to create a new file.

To create a new file using the default layout:

◆   Click the **New** tool ⬜ on the Standard toolbar.

A new file will appear, e.g. Document2, Book2, (the number in the file name depends on the number of files you have created in this working session).

Open a file

If you want to view, update or print a file that you have already created, saved and closed you must open the file that you want to work with.

To open an existing file:

❶   Click the **Open** tool ⬜ on the Standard toolbar. The **Open** dialog box will appear on your screen.

❷   Locate the drive and/or folder in which your file is stored.

❸   Select the file you wish to open – click on its name.

❹   Click **Open**.

◆   You can also open a file by double clicking on its name in the **Open** dialog box.

If the file you want to open is a recently used one you will find its name displayed at the bottom of the File menu. You can open your file from here, rather than go through the **Open** dialog box.

❶   Open the **File** menu.

❷   Click on the file name you want to open.

If you have more than one file open, you will see the filenames displayed on the Taskbar at the bottom of your screen. If you point to the filename on the Taskbar, the full file name and the name of the application will be displayed. To move from one file to another, click on the file name that you want to display.

◆   You can also use the **Window** menu in an application to go from one open file to another – you will find a list of your open files at the end of it. Just click on the one you want to display.

If you wish to open more than one file simultaneously, select the files in the **Open** dialog box, then click **Open**.

Select files

To select a group of adjacent files:

❶   Click on the first file or folder.

❷   Hold the [Shift] key down.

❸   Click on the last file or folder.

To select several non-adjacent files:

❶   Click on the first file or folder.

❷   Hold the [Ctrl] key down.

❸   Click on each of the other files or folders as required.

8.4 MS Office Help!

As you work with your applications you will most probably find that you come a bit unstuck from time to time and need help! There are several ways of getting help – most of them very intuitive and user friendly. The Help system works in the same way in all Office applications.

Office Assistant

To call on the Office Assistant, press [F1] or click the application **Help** tool 🔲 on the toolbar.

Depending on what you have been doing, the Assistant may display a list of topics that you might be interested in.

- To choose a topic from the 'What would you like to do?' list, simply click on the topic.

- If you have a specific question you want to ask, type it in at the prompt and click the **Search** button.

- The Assistant will display the Help page.

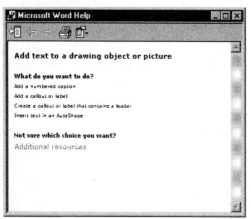

Some Help pages contain text in a different coloured font – usually blue. If the text is part of a list at the top of a help page it indicates a link to a different area of the current Help page. If the coloured text is embedded within the main text on a page it is probably a phrase or some jargon that has an explanation or definition attached to it. Simply click the coloured text to display the definition. Any related Help pages will be cross-referenced at the end of the page – to display a related page simply click on its cross-reference.

- Links that have been used change colour – typically to violet.

- When you've finished exploring the Help system, click the **Close** button at the top right of the Help window.

The Office Assistant can remain visible as you work on your document, or you can hide it and call on it as required. If you opt to leave it displayed, drag it to an area of your screen where it doesn't obscure your work.

♦ If you leave the Office Assistant displayed, left click on it any time you want to ask a question.

♦ To hide the Office Assistant, right click on it and choose **Hide** from the pop up menu. To show it again, open the **Help** menu and choose **Show the Office Assistant**.

♦ To change the way the Office assistant works, right click on it and choose **Options** from the pop up menu. Set the options required in the **Office Assistant** dialog box.

Tips

The Office Assistant is constantly monitoring your actions. If it thinks that it has a tip that may be useful to you, a light bulb will light up beside it. To read its tip, click the bulb.

What's This?

If you haven't used Microsoft Office products before, or if you're new to the Windows environment, there will be many tools, menus, buttons and areas on your screen that puzzle you. The *What's This?* feature can help you here – it works best when a file is open, as most of the tools, menus and screen areas are then active.

To find out what a tool does:

❶ Hold down the [Shift] key and press [F1].

❷ Click the tool.

To find out about an item in a menu list:

❶ Hold down the [Shift] key and press [F1].

❷ Open the menu list and select the option required from the list.

To find out about anything else within the application window:

❶ Hold down the [Shift] key and press [F1].

❷ Click on the item.

If you accidentally invoke the *What's This* help option, press [Shift]-[F1] (or the [Esc] key) to cancel it.

Contents and Index

Whether or not you opt to use the Office Assistant, the application Help tool  will open the on-line Help system. You can also access the system from the **Help** menu.

If you access the Help system through the Office Assistant, the Help page requested is displayed on the screen.

- You can interrogate the Help system using the Contents, Answer Wizard or Index tabs.

- Click the tool to toggle the display of the tabs.

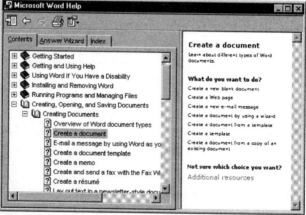

Contents Tab

You can 'browse' through the Help system from the Contents tab. Click the + to the left of a book to display or the − to hide its list of contents.

When a book is open, you will be presented with a list of topics.

To display a topic:

❶   Click on it.

❷   Work through the system until you find the help you need.

To print a topic:

◆   Click the **Print** tool 🖨 in the **Help** window when the topic is displayed.

To revisit pages you've already been to:

◆   Click the **Back** tool ⇦ or **Forward** tool ⇨ to go back and forward through the pages.

Close the Help window when you've finished.

Answer Wizard

If you want to interrogate the help system by asking a question, try the Answer Wizard tab.

❶   Enter your question, e.g. *How do I create a table* and click **Search**.

❷   Select a topic from the **Select topic to display** list.

◆   The Help page will be displayed.

Index Tab

If you know what you are looking for, the Index tab gives you quick access to any topic and is particularly useful once you are familiar with the terminology used in your application.

❶   At the **Help** dialog box, select the **Index** tab.

❷   Type the word you're looking for in the *Type keywords* field and click **Search**.

Or

❸   Double click on a word in the **Or choose keywords** list.

❹   Choose a topic from the **Choose a topic** list.

❺   Work through the help system until you find what you are looking for.

❻   Close the **Help** window when you've finished.

ScreenTips

If you point to any tool on a displayed toolbar, a ScreenTip will probably appear to describe the purpose of the tool.

If no ScreenTips appear, you can easily switch them on if you want to.

To switch ScreenTips on or off:

❶ Point to any toolbar that is displayed and click the right mouse button.

❷ Choose **Customize...** from the shortcut menu.

❸ In the **Customize** dialog box select the **Options** tab.

❹ To switch ScreenTips on, select the **Show ScreenTips on toolbars** option (if you don't like ScreenTips, deselect this option).

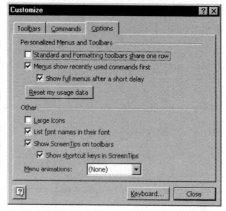

❺ Click **Close**.

Dialog box Help

When you access a dialog box in an application, e.g. the Customize one above, you can get help on any item within it that you don't understand. To get help on an item in a dialog box:

❶ Click the [?] help button at the right of the dialog box title bar.

❷ Click on an option, button or item that you want explained. A brief explanation of it will be displayed.

❸ Click anywhere within the dialog box to close the explanation display.

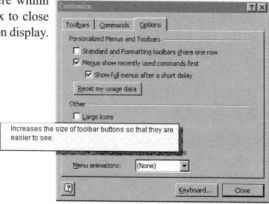

8.5 Delete, Cut, Copy and Paste

Delete

If you have a large piece of text or data to delete, it will usually be quicker to select it and then press [Delete], rather than press [←] or [Delete] repetitively.

To delete a chunk of text or data

❶ Select it.

❷ Press [Delete].

Cut, Copy and Paste

There will be times when you have entered the correct information into a file but it is in the wrong place. When this happens you should move or copy the object, e.g. text in Word, data in cells in Excel, a picture or graph in any application, to the correct location.

- If you want to remove an object from its current position, and place it somewhere else, you can *move* it from one place to another.

- If you want to keep the object, but repeat it in another place in your file (or in another file), you can *copy* it.

You can move or copy an object within or between files. Before you can move or copy something you must select it.

Move (cut) or copy (copy) and paste

❶ Select the object that you want to move.

❷ Click the **Cut** tool ✂ to move or the **Copy** tool ⧉ to copy (they're on the Standard toolbar).

❸ Position the insertion point where you want the object to reappear.

❹ Click the **Paste** tool ⧉ on the Standard toolbar.

- The object will appear at the insertion point.

Cut or Copy to a different file

To move or copy an object from one file to another:

❶ Open the file you want to move or copy the object from (the source file).

❷ Open the file you want to move or copy the object to (the destination file).

❸ Display the file you want to move or copy from.

❹ Select the object you want to move or copy.

❺ Click the **Cut** ✄ or **Copy** tool 📋 on the Standard toolbar.

❻ Display the file you want to move or copy the object to.

❼ Position the insertion point where you want the object to go.

❽ Click the **Paste** tool 📋 on the Standard toolbar.

Drag and drop

As an alternative to using Cut or Copy and Paste techniques to move and copy objects, you may find *drag and drop* useful.

Drag and drop is especially useful when moving or copying an object a short distance – i.e. to somewhere else on the screen. If you try to drag and drop over a longer distance, you will probably find that your file scrolls very quickly on the screen and that it is very difficult to control.

To move or copy:

❶ Select the object that you want to move or copy.

❷ Position the mouse pointer anywhere over the selected object.

To move the text:

❸ Click and hold down the left mouse button (notice the 'ghost' insertion point that appears within the selected area).

❹ Drag the object and 'drop' it into its new position.

To copy the text:

❸ Hold down your [Ctrl] key.

❹ Click and hold down the left mouse button (notice the 'ghost' insertion point that appears within the selected area).

❺ Drag the object and 'drop' it into its new position .

❻ Let go the [Ctrl] key.

8.6 Spelling and grammar

To help you produce accurate work, you can check the spelling and grammar in your document. You can either:

♦ Let the application check your spelling and grammar as you work (Word and PowerPoint).

Or

♦ Run a spell-check at a time that suits you (all applications).

Checking spelling and grammar as you type

This option is operational by default – if it doesn't work on your system, someone has switched it off.

♦ Words that aren't recognized will be underlined with a red, wavy line.

♦ Any words, phrases or sentences that have unusual capitalization or aren't grammatically correct will have a grey wavy line.

Spelling errors – to find out what Word or PowerPoint suggests as an alternative, click the right mouse button on the highlighted word.

♦ If you wish to change the word in your document to one of those listed, left click on the word that you want to use in the shortcut menu.

♦ If you choose **Ignore All**, the word will not be highlighted again in the document in this working session.

♦ If you choose **Add**, the word will be added to the dictionary, and it will be recognized as a correctly spelt word from now on.

Grammatical errors – can be dealt with in a similar way. When you right click on the error, the application will display the problem, and suggest a remedy if it can. You can choose whether you wish to change your text to that suggested or ignore the suggestion.

Checking spelling and grammar when you are ready

You can easily check your spelling and grammar at any time using the **Spelling and Grammar** tool on the Standard toolbar.

To start checking:

❶ Click the **Spelling and Grammar** tool .

♦ The application will spell check your file. Respond to the prompts as you see fit. When the checking is complete, a prompt will appear to tell you so.

❷ Click **OK** to return to your file.

8.7   Font formatting

One way of enhancing your text is to apply font formatting to it. These effects can be applied to individual characters in your file. The most commonly used font formatting options have tools on the Formatting toolbar – other options can be found in the **Format**, **Font** dialog box. The Formatting toolbar varies a little from application to application – this one is from Word. The formatting options discussed here are available in *all* Office applications.

To format text or data as you type it in:

❶ Switch on the formatting option(s) required.

❷ Type in the text or data.

❸ Switch off or change the formatting option.

To apply formatting to/change the formatting of existing text or data:

❶ Select the text or data.

❷ Switch the formatting option required on or off, or apply an additional format.

Bold, italic and underline

♦ To switch bold on or off, click the **Bold** tool B .

♦ To switch italic on or off, click the *Italic* tool I .

♦ To switch underline on or off, click the Underline tool U .

Font styles, size and colour

The font style, size and colour are also easily changed.

To change the style of font:

❶ Click the drop down arrow to the right of the **Font** tool on the For-matting toolbar.

❷ Scroll through the list of available fonts until you see the font you want to use.

❸ Click on it.

To change the size of font:

❶ Click the drop down arrow to the right of the **Font Size** tool on the Formatting toolbar.

❷ Scroll through the list of available sizes and click on the one you want to use.

To change the colour of font:

❶ Click the drop down arrow to the right of the **Font Color** tool on the Formatting toolbar to display the Font Color toolbar.

❷ Select the colour you want to use.

8.8 Paragraph/cell formatting

The default paragraph (Word/PowerPoint) or cell (Excel/Access) format-ting options gives you a left-aligned text, with single line spacing. If this is not the formatting you require you can change it.

To apply formatting to a paragraph or cell as you type:

❶ Set the formatting option required.

❷ Enter your text.

To apply formatting to existing text:

❶ Select the text or cell(s).

❷ Apply the formatting required.

Alignment

To **centre** a paragraph, or text or data within a cell

* Click the **Centre** tool ▤ on the Formatting toolbar.

To **justify** a paragraph (or paragraphs):

* Click the **Justify** tool ▤ on the Formatting toolbar.

To **right align** a paragraph (or paragraphs) or text or data within a cell:

* Click the **Align Right** ▤ tool on the Formatting toolbar.

To **left align** a paragraph (or paragraphs) or text or data within a cell:

* Click the **Align Left** tool ▤ on the Formatting toolbar.

Borders and shading

Borders and shading are also paragraph or cell formatting options that can be very useful when it comes to emphasizing areas in your file.

To place a border around paragraph(s) or cell(s):

❶ Select the paragraph(s) or cell(s).

❷ Click the drop down arrow to the right of the **Borders** tool to display the Borders toolbar.

❸ Select the border required from the options available.

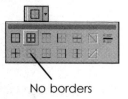

No borders

To remove a border from paragraph(s) or cells:

❶ Select the paragraph(s) or cell(s) you want to remove borders from.

❷ Display the **Borders** toolbar.

❸ Click the **No Border** tool.

There are more options in the **Borders and Shading** dialog box. You can apply a border to all four sides (an outside border) using the Box, Shadow or 3-D setting.

❶ Open the **Format** menu and choose **Borders and Shading...**

❷ Experiment with the options.

❸ Click **OK** or **Cancel** (depending on whether or not you wish to apply the formats you have selected).

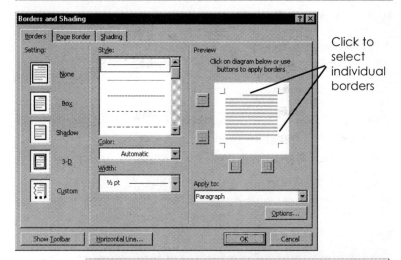

Click to
select
individual
borders

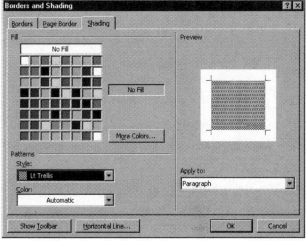

To switch individual borders (left, right, top or bottom) on and off, click the border tools in the **Preview** window, or the lines around the edges of the example in the **Preview** window.

You can choose a shading effect for your paragraph(s) or cell(s). Select the **Shading** tab and explore the options.

8.9   Format Painter

If you need to apply the same formatting to different pieces of text through-
out your document, you could use the Format Painter to 'paint' the formatting onto your text.

To use the Format Painter:

❶   Select some text or data that has been formatted using the options you
       want to 'paint' onto other text.

❷   Click the **Format Painter** tool 🖌.

❸   Click and drag over the text you want to 'paint' the formatting on to.

◆   If you want to paint the formats onto several separate pieces of
    text, lock the Format Painter on by double clicking on it.When you
    have finished, click the Format Painter tool again to unlock it.

8.10   Undo

To undo an action:

◆   Click the **Undo** tool 🔄 on the Standard toolbar.

Or

◆   Press [Ctrl]-[Z].

If you undo something by mistake, and want to redo it:

◆   Click the **Redo** tool 🔁 on the Standard toolbar.

8.11   Preview and Print

At some stage you will want to print your file. I suggest you *preview* it
first. The preview will display a full page of your file on the screen at once
(more than one page if you wish) so that you can check how the finished
page will look. Basic preview and print options are given here – any that
are specific to each application are discussed in the relevant chapters.

Print Preview

◆   To preview your document, click the **Print Preview** tool 🔍 on the
    Standard toolbar.

A full-page preview of your document will appear on screen and the Print Preview toolbar for the application will be displayed.

To print one copy of your file to the default printer:

♦   Click the **Print** tool  on the Standard or Print Preview toolbar.

Printing to another installed printer:

❶   Open the **File** menu and choose **Print**.

❷   Select the printer required in the **Name field**.

❸   Set other options as required.

❹   Click **OK**.

To print to file

If you don't have a printer attached to your computer, or if you want to print your file out on a computer that doesn't have the application that you are using on it, you can print to a file. The file can then be printed out on any PC.

❶   Open the **File** menu and choose **Print**.

❷   In the **Name** field select the printer that will be used to print the file.

❸   Select the **Print to file** check box.

❹   Click **OK**.

❺   In the **Print to file** dialog box, select the drive and or folder if necessary, give your file a name and click **OK**.

8.12   Drawings

You can easily draw shapes and create images in your files using the Drawing toolbar. If the Drawing toolbar isn't displayed, you need to display it.

To display the Drawing toolbar:

♦   Click the **Drawing** tool on the Standard toolbar.

To draw a line, arrow, rectangle or oval:

❶ Click the line, arrow, rectangle or oval tool on the Drawing toolbar.

❷ Click and drag where you want 'draw' your shape.

To draw a square or circle:

❶ Select the rectangle or oval tool on the Drawing toolbar.

❷ Click at the position you want the shape.

To enter an AutoShape:

❶ Click the **AutoShapes** tool on the Drawing toolbar.

❷ Pick a category.

❸ Select a shape.

❹ Click at the position you want the shape.

To add a text box:

❶ Select the **Text Box** tool.

❷ Click at the position you want the text box.

❸ Type in your text.

WordArt

WordArt gives you the option of creating special text effects in your file.

❶ Click the Insert **WordArt** tool 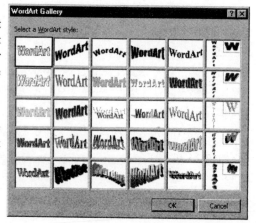 on the Drawing toolbar.

❷ Select a WordArt style as required from the **Gallery**.

❸ Click **OK**.

❹ At the **Edit WordArt Text** dialog box, enter (and format) the text.

❺ Click **OK**.

❻ Adjust the shape of your WordArt object as required.

The WordArt toolbar

* Experiment with the tools to see the effects they produce.

Formatting drawing objects

If a drawing object is *selected* it has handles at each corner/along each side (squares).

A selected object can be moved, resized or deleted. You can also change the line styles, add a fill colour or special effect.

To move a shape	Place mouse pointer within the shape and click and drag
To resize a shape	Place mouse pointer over a handle and click and drag
To delete a shape	Press [Delete]
To change line style	Click the **Line Style** tool and choose a style
To change line colour	Click the arrow beside the **Line Colour** field and pick one
To change the fill colour	Click the arrow beside the **Fill Color** tool and choose a colour
To add a shadow	Click the **Shadow** tool and select an effect
To add a 3-D effect	Click the **3-D effect** tool and choose from the options available

8.13 Pictures

If you've installed Microsoft Office you'll find you've access to lots of Clip Art. If you've Internet access, you'll also find lots of Clip Art online.

To insert Clip Art

❶ Click the **Insert Clip Art** tool [img] on the Drawing toolbar.

❷ Select a category in the **Insert ClipArt** dialog box – click on one.

❸   Scroll through the clips and select the one you want to use.

❹   Click the **Preview clip** tool to magnify the image if you want a closer look at it.

❺   Click the **Insert clip** tool to place the image in your document.

❻   Close the **Insert ClipArt** dialog box.

The clip you have inserted can be resized, moved or deleted using the same techniques as with drawings.

◆   Double click on the clip to open the **Format Picture** dialog box to gain access to all the formatting options for the object.

To search for clips

If you find scrolling through the clips in the **Insert ClipArt** dialog box a bit tedious, you can always use the **Find...** options to locate clip art that may be suitable.

❶   Open the **Insert ClipArt** dialog box.

❷   Enter the keyword you're looking for, e.g. sunshine, in the search for clips field.

❸   Press [Enter].

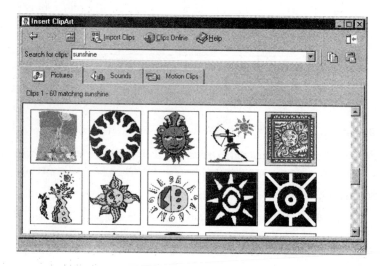

The clips that you insert into your document can be formatted in a number of ways – the best thing to do is experiment.

When a clip is selected the Picture toolbar is displayed. You can use the toolbar to modify your picture.

The Picture toolbar

Working from left to right on the toolbar:

Insert Picture – inserts a picture *from File* rather than from the Gallery.

Image Control – *Automatic* is the default; *Greyscale* converts each colour to a different shade of grey; *Black and white* converts the picture to a black and white picture; *Watermark* converts the object to a low contrast picture that you can place behind everything else to create a watermark.

More Contrast – increase the contrast.

Less Contrast – decrease the contrast.

More Brightness – increase the brightness.

Less Brightness – decrease the brightness.

Crop – lets you trim the edges off the clip.

To crop a clip:

❶   Select it.

❷   Click the **Crop** tool.

❸   Drag a resizing handle to crop (cut off) the bits you don't want.

Line Style – put lines around the picture, or change the line style used.

Text Wrapping – lets you specify how text should wrap around a picture.

Format Picture – opens the **Format Picture** dialog box where you have access to even more formatting options.

Set Transparent Color – used to integrate a picture on your page. For bitmaps, JPEGs and GIFs that don't have transparency information, and also for some clip art.

Reset Picture – returns the clip to its original state.

If you have pictures on disk that are not in the Gallery (perhaps a photograph you've scanned in), you can still insert them into your document.

To insert a picture from a file:

❶ Open the **Insert** menu.

❷ Select **Picture**.

❸ Choose **From File...**

❹ Locate the file you want to insert – explore the folders on your system.

❺ Select the file and click **Insert**.

8.14 Toolbars

Showing and hiding toolbars

You may have noticed that some toolbars appear and disappear automatically as you work in an application. The Picture toolbar appears when a Clip Art object selected, the WordArt toolbar appears when a WordArt object is selected.

You can opt to show or hide toolbars whenever you want to use the tools on them. Provided you have at least one toolbar displayed, you can use the shortcut method to show or hide any toolbar.

To use the shortcut method:

❶ Point to a toolbar.

❷ Click the right mouse button.

◆ Any toolbars that are displayed have a tick beside their name, any that are not displayed have no tick.

❸ Click (using the *left* mouse button) on the toolbar name you wish to show or hide.

If no toolbars are displayed, you must use the **View** menu to show them again.

❶ Open the **View** menu and choose **Toolbars**.

❷ Click on the one you want to show.

Using either of the methods above, you can show or hide one toolbar at a time. If you want to change the display status of several toolbars at the one time, it may be quicker to use the **Customize** dialog box.

❶   Right click on a toolbar that is currently displayed.

Or

♦   Open the **View** menu and choose **Toolbars**.

❷   Click **Customize...**

❸   On the **Toolbars** tab, select or deselect the toolbars as required (a tick means they are displayed, no tick means they are hidden).

❹   Click **Close**.

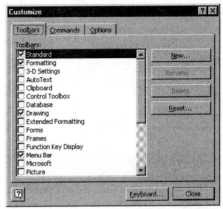

Moving toolbars

Toolbars can be positioned *anywhere* on your screen. There are four *docking* areas – at the top, bottom, left and right of your screen, and your toolbars can be placed in any of them. You can also leave your toolbar floating in the document area if you prefer.

The Standard and Formatting toolbars are normally displayed along the top of your screen, docked side by side, sharing one row.

If the toolbar is docked:

❶   Point to the left edge of the toolbar (if the toolbar is docked at the top or bottom of the screen) or top edge (if the toolbar is docked at the left or right of the screen) – where the two raised lines are.

❷   Drag and drop the toolbar to the position you want it in.

If the toolbar is not docked

❶   Point to its Title bar.

❷   Drag and drop the toolbar to the position you want it in.

If you don't want the Standard and Formatting toolbar to share one row, you can switch off the option that enables this feature. The Standard and

Formatting toolbars can then be positioned as they were in previous versions of Office – the Standard one above the Formatting one.

To disable the row sharing option:

❶ Right click a toolbar that is currently displayed.

Or

♦ Choose **Toolbars** from the **View** menu.

❷ Click on **Customize...**

❸ Select the **Options** tab.

❹ De-select the Standard and Formatting toolbars share one row checkbox.

❺ Click **Close**.

SUMMARY

This chapter discussed features that can be used in any of the applications in Office. These features included:

✓ Opening and closing an application.

✓ File handling – New, Open, Close, Save, Save As.

✓ On-line Help.

✓ Delete, Cut, Copy and Paste.

✓ Spell & Grammar checker.

✓ Formatting – font and paragraph/cell.

✓ Format painter.

✓ Preview & Print.

✓ Drawing toolbar.

✓ Pictures – ClipArt.

✓ Show, hide and move toolbars.

INDEX